£8

FORT JESUS OF MOMBASA

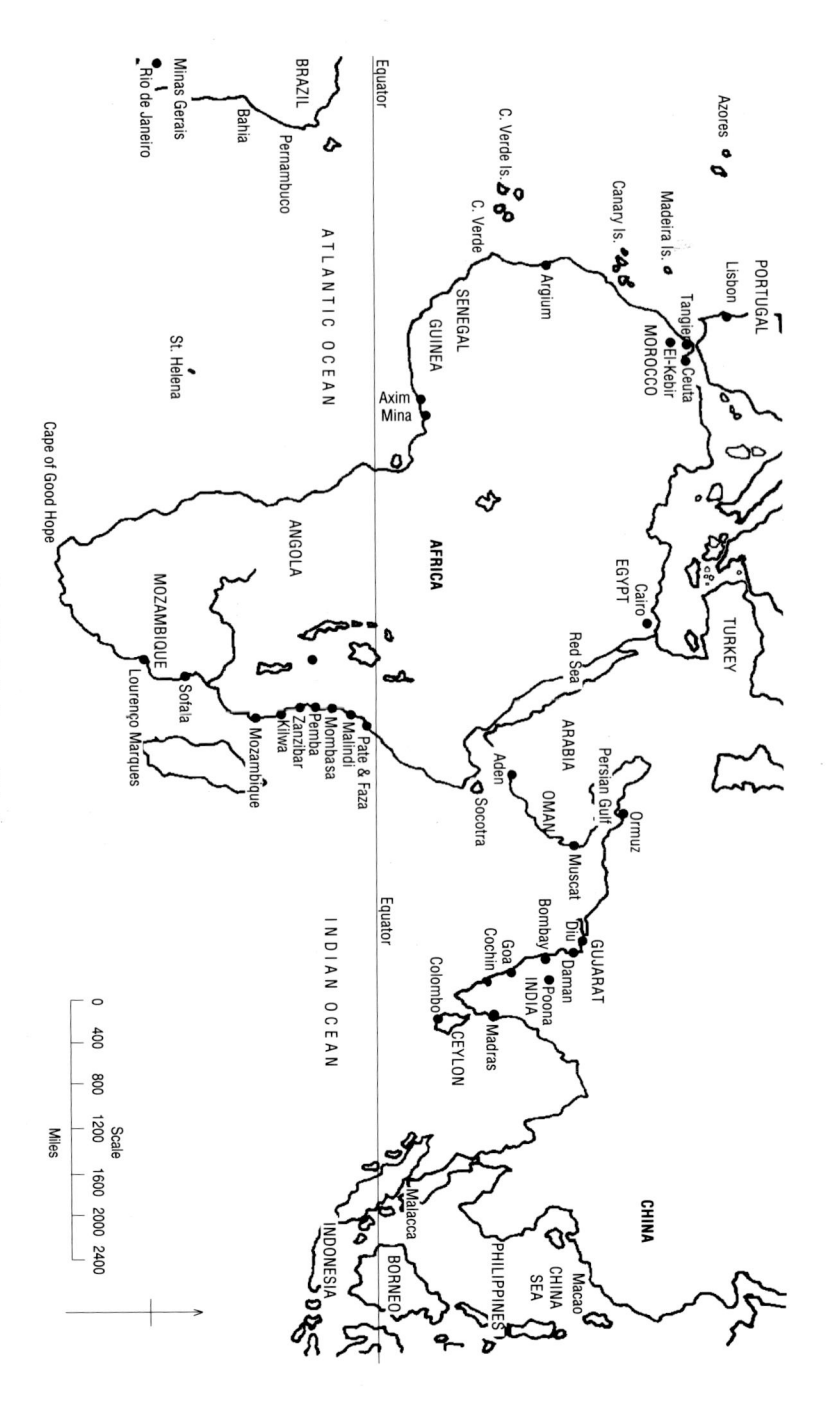

Map 1 Africa, Indian Ocean and China Sea

FORT JESUS
of MOMBASA

W. A. Nelson

CANONGATE PRESS

First published in 1994 by Canongate Press PLC
14 Frederick Street, Edinburgh EH2 2HB

Copyright © W A Nelson 1994

ISBN: 0 86241 393 1

All rights reserved
The right of W A Nelson to be identified as the
author of this work has been asserted by him in accordance with
the Copyright Design and Patent Act 1988.

British Library Cataloguing-in-Publication Data.
A catalogue record for this book is available from
the British Library.

Typesetting by Hewer Text Composition Services, Edinburgh
Printed and bound by Hong Kong Reprohouse

CONTENTS

	Page
List of Maps	vi
List of Plans	vi
List of Figures	vii
Preface	9
Introduction	11
FORT JESUS	
Design and History	17
Description	30
Conclusion	51
MALINDI AND GEDI	56
Appendices	
A Cannon and cannon balls	64
B Gun embrasures and loopholes	67
C Stone sentry-boxes	69
D Artillery fortification terms	71
E Fort S Sebastian, Mozambique	73
Bibliography	79
Index	81

LIST OF MAPS

Number		Page
1	Africa, Indian Ocean and China Sea	Frontispiece
2	Eastern Africa, Oman and Persian Gulf	17

LIST OF PLANS

Number		Page
1	Fort Jesus, as at present	Front end paper
2	Fort Jesus, before 1635	22
3	Fort Jesus, after 1635	26
4	Fort George (Scotland), outworks	53
5	Fort Jesus, stone sentry boxes	69
6	Fort S Sebastian, Mozambique	74

LIST OF FIGURES

Number		Page
	INTRODUCTION	
	Construction of bastion/rampart fort	
1	Earthworks, section	15
2	Finished plan	16
3	Completed works, section	16
	FORT JESUS	
	General	
4	Parapets, as originally built	19
5	Parapets, as should have been built	20
6	Harbour front	20
	Description	
7	Northern entrance front	30
8	S Filipe, recessed flank	31
9	S Alberto, west face and ditch	32
10	S Alberto, east flank and south rampart	33
11	East end of south ditch	34
12	S Mateus, postern and coral cutting	35
13	Outwork, gun-embrasure	36
14	Outwork and rectangular projection	37
15	Outwork, projection and S Matias	37
16	S Matias, east face	38
17	Outer gate, from depression	39
18	Church foundations, end-on	39
19	Cistern, rear	41
20	Museum and gun barrels	41
21	North rampart, gatehouse and gun barrels	42
22	Mazrui house, end view	43
23	Passage of Arches, slope down	44
24	Arab doorway	45

Number		Page
25	Rectangular projection, battlements	46
26	North rampart and barracks	46
27	South rampart, parapet interior	47
28	S Mateus, east face loophole	48
29	*Pegasus* guns	49
	Conclusion	
30	Fort George (Scotland), ravelin	52
	MALINDI AND GEDI	
31	Vasco da Gama Street, Mombasa	56
32	Fruit market, Mombasa	57
33	Moslem mosque, Mombasa	57
34	Kenyan seashore	58
35	Vasco da Gama's pillar at Malindi	59
36	Gedi, the Palace Gate	60
37	Gedi, house gateway	61
38	Gedi, house remains and well	61
39	Gedi, pillar tomb	62
40	Gedi, tree splitting wall	63
	APPENDIX E	
41	S Sebastian, harbour gate approach	75
42	S Sebastian, chapel	76

Note: Illustrations are by the writer, except for those given below, which are reproduced with the kind permission of those named – who are the copyright holders.
Nos 17, 41, 42   Dr J.S. Kirkman
Nos 6, 13, 31, 32, 33, 34   Frank Ltd, Mombasa
No 30   The Scottish Development Department.

PREFACE

There is much to be said for the validity of first impressions. Until September 1986 I had never been in Mombasa or, indeed, in any other place in the vast continent of Africa. The first view I had, therefore, of the entry front of Fort Jesus was the first time I had looked upon it. The impressions were clear. They were of brooding, massive strength and of a dark red colour. A second glance showed that the plaster that covered all the exterior was not red but in part yellow-ochre and in part light grey.

Nevertheless, the impression of the dark colour of blood remained.

It is right that it should so remain, since over the centuries Fort Jesus has had a bloodstained history. While it has certainly had its loyalties and its acts of courage, it has also had its betrayals and massacres. It has also been unusual among fortresses in that, since it was founded just before the year 1600, it has never been unoccupied (except for a few weeks in 1632) and that it has been the centre of political power upon the East African coast for a succession of rulers, both Portuguese and Arab. It is now one of the principal historical monuments upon the coast of the Republic of Kenya.

It was with extreme hesitation that I began an account of Fort Jesus, for this has already been done, in most masterly fashion, by a number of distinguished scholars, to whose works can be added little. Chief among those scholars is the noted Dr J. S. Kirkman, (who, sadly, died in 1989) the doyen among East African historians and archaeologists and, for many years, the resident Curator of the Fort and its Museum. After his *Fort Jesus. A Portuguese Fortress upon the East African Coast* published in 1974, there can be very little for anyone else to say. In addition, the equally noted British historian, Professor C. R. Boxer, was a joint author in 1960 with the Portuguese scholar Dr Carlos de Azevedo of *Fort Jesus and the Portuguese in Mombasa*. Nevertheless, at a much more ordinary and pedestrian level, there may still be room for an account by someone who was really little more than a passing visitor. Thus this book has limitations, in that it has been written for the general reader rather than for scholars. However, there is a proper place for the general reader.

This record can, in no way, substitute for the work of previous authors but it might perhaps slightly supplement it. There are, in addition, a number of appendices on specific subjects.

There is an additional and important reason for writing this book. It is sometimes implied that European colonial forts are slight and weak and not to be compared for strength with their counterparts in Europe. This is not so, as is demonstrated by the well built and up-to-date works – both forts and fortified towns – constructed by the Portuguese, Spanish, Dutch, French and British. The two Portuguese forts described here (Jesus at Mombasa and, in an appendix, S Sebastian at Mozambique) are as powerful as are their home contemporaries. Furthermore, they are properly representative of colonial forts as a whole. These were not restricted to the bastion trace but passed also into the later realms of the polygonal fort and the tenaille trace. There may possibly be a case, in this country, for studying more extensively the whole range of colonial fortifications.

In the preparation of this book, absolutely essential assistance was received from many generous persons. Dr Kirkman, in addition to reading the manuscript and correcting its mistakes, was most liberal in his helpful advice. The other reader of the manuscript was the leading British authority on artillery fortification, Dr Quentin Hughes, formerly of Liverpool University. They both gave advice and corrections of the utmost value. Professor C. R. Boxer most generously gave of his profound knowledge of all things Portuguese. Professor Roy Bridges, of Aberdeen University, lent key books of reference and also gave essential advice and introductions. Professor Geoffrey Parker, of the University of Illinois, made most helpful comments. The late Mr James de Vere Allen, a distinguished Kenyan academic historian, gave most useful information. The senior officials at Fort Jesus, that is to say, the Curator, Mr Ali Abubakar, the Director of Coastal Museums, Mr Osman Bwana, and the Museum Education Officer, Mr Abdul Mwinzagu, could not possibly have been more co-operative and friendly. Their provision of a room and a desk was of especial assistance as an antidote to the tropical sun and intense heat when I was working around the Fort. My gratitude for manuscript reading goes also to my sister and brother and to Mr John Plant. Finally, my thanks are given to Sandra Bruce for the perfect manner in which she dealt with a not always easy manuscript. Needless to say, any remaining errors are mine alone, as are opinions expressed.

W. A. Nelson
Aberdeen 1993

INTRODUCTION

We in Britain have tended to ignore both the good fighting qualities of the Portuguese infantry when well led, as it was by Wellington during his victorious Peninsular War, and also the extent and the longevity of the Portuguese overseas empire.

Scholars of outstanding eminence such as Professor C. R. Boxer (*The Portuguese Seaborne Empire 1415–1825*), have analysed these questions in great detail and with deep understanding of, and sympathy for, the Portuguese character and history, both in their home country and overseas. It is perhaps illuminating that the last chapter of his book on their empire deals with Portuguese mysticism.

Mysticism and religion are not the same thing, although they are inter-related. It is not altogether easy for us in Britain today, with the basically secular society in which we live, to comprehend that, for many others, it is religion that matters most. Thus it was for the Portuguese in their days of empire from shortly after the year AD 1400 until almost the present day. In addition to trade, national pride and strategic advantages, it was religious faith – the Catholic Christian faith – that enabled the Portuguese empire for so long to withstand the buffetings of nature and of more powerful colonial rivals.

Portugal was a small, poor country. Yet the Portuguese had been given one great gift by nature. They had shared with the rest of the western fringe of Europe in the gales and storms driven in by the Atlantic westerly winds. This made them tough and hardy sailors. They shared with the Spaniards the expulsion of the Moors from the Iberian Peninsula. So the harsh material of conquest had been forged. Portugal's Moslem foe lay in Morocco. That conquest began with the capture in 1415 of the Moslem town of Ceuta on the Moroccan side of the Straits of Gibraltar.

From this start, commenced an astonishing series of voyages and explorations down the almost endless side of the west of Africa. In those journeys, the Portuguese discovered also the uninhabited offshore islands of the Azores, Madeira, the Canaries and Cape Verdes. In the course of that, they learned about deep-sea navigation, ocean winds and sea currents. From that, they came to realise that they might be able to sail round all Africa. The man who masterminded this grand scheme was Prince Henry of the ruling house of Aviz. By the time the Prince died in 1460, the Portuguese royal empire was established, with its first land forts in West Africa founded at Arguim in about 1445 and with later forts at A Mina and Axim, all along the coast of Guinea and Senegal (Map 1). From those forts, gold and African slaves could be shipped back to Lisbon, to help defray the mounting costs of the new empire.

The push southwards along the lower part of the western African coast, often bleak, often barren, continued. During the last decade of the 1400s, first Bartholomue Diaz followed that coast until it turned northwards and then Vasco da Gama crossed the Indian Ocean to reach the Malabar coast of India. The potential Christian ally, the wholly mythical Prester John in Abyssinia, was now thought to be within reach and willing to fall upon the North African Moslem states from the rear.

From this period onwards until the end of the sailing era in the 1800s, a series of European nations were to establish colonial mastery in turn. First, it was to be Portugal's century of such mastery, the years from 1500 to 1600.

How did a small, poor country like Portugal do it? The answer is that, in addition to religious drive and desire for trade, they were the first western nation to achieve the marriage of the strongly-built sailing ship with the heavy cannon firing broadside. That lethal combination was to influence world domination until the 1800s.

That lethal combination was also achieved by the Spaniards at about the same time. However, as they went west across the Atlantic and not to the east, their story does not enter into this account.

During the 1400s gunpowder and cannon were steadily putting out of date the earlier methods of sea warfare by ramming and boarding from swift, but lightly-built oar and sail galleys. Those could not house an adequate complement of cannon and it was to be the strong sailing ship alone that could do so. Again, exploration and long journeys across the open seas required not lean galleys incapable of carrying substantial stocks of food and water but large solid ships with plenty of hold space. Thus, the mastery of the oceans passed from the Mediterranean powers, both Christian and Moslem, and fell into the hands of the Portuguese.

The latter had not arrived in the Indian Ocean for purposes of peace but to offer the non-Christians they encountered the alternatives of conversion to Christianity or death. Fundamentally, which it was to be turned upon comparative armaments, not upon philosophies or discussions. First such Moslem Arab and, later, such Moslem Egyptian and Turkish fleets as sailed to oppose them were blown away and the Portuguese were left to range the Indian Ocean at their will.

The Portuguese were fortunate, not only in the timing of their arrival in the Indian Ocean, but also in the personalities of some of their early leaders. These could see that, despite their invincibility at sea, their small numbers made them highly vulnerable upon land. So they secured their position in the Indian Ocean by the seizing of a number of key land bases; Mozambique guarding the entry from the west; Ormuz blocking the Persian Gulf; Goa in the centre of India's western Malabar coast and Malacca, controlling the trade with China and Japan. Only at Aden did they fail in 1513 to capture a port to block the Red Sea.

Although their failure at Aden prevented their command of the Indian Ocean from being complete, the other places gave them control of the valuable spice trade of Indonesia, the Arab horse trade and the African Zambesi gold trade.

To the east of Malacca, the Portuguese penetrations was more that of another trader rather than that of a conqueror, for in the China Sea the Chinese war junks twice defeated them in 1521 and 1522. They did succeed in setting up a trading base in China, at Macao fifteen years later. It was to Brazil only that the Portuguese travelled westwards. There they set up a number of widely-spaced settlements on the jungle-covered and fever-ridden coasts. Those for a long time were more a financial liability than an asset, until in about 1690 gold and diamonds were found near Rio de Janeiro. Thereafter, Brazilian wealth was to pour into Lisbon.

Although Portugal appeared to be riding on the crest of the colonial wave, certain vital shortages in men, money, ships, cannon, timber and marriageable European women were already showing, shortages that in the end would bring down the whole structure of the Portuguese royal empire.

That decline was much hastened by a military disaster close at home in Morocco. In 1578, an ailing, unwise and childless king led an ill-organised expedition across the Straits. This army was destroyed at El-Kasr-el-Kebir and the king was killed. Thereupon, King Philip II of Spain, who had a legitimate claim, though his mother, to the Crown of Portugal, invaded his neighbour and conquered her. This brought Portugal into conflict with the Protestant Dutch, who were locked in a long war with Catholic Spain. The Dutch fell with vigour upon the overseas possessions of Catholic Portugal. The result might perhaps broadly be called a draw. In Indonesia, coastal Ceylon and along the southern part of the Malabar coast of India the Portuguese were driven out. At Macao and Mozambique the Dutch were repulsed. In Angola the Portuguese won as did he Duch in the West African bulge. In

Brazil, the Dutch first won but later lost. To preserve themselves, the Portuguese were obliged to make a marriage alliance with Britain, under which Tangier and Bombay were unwillingly ceded as part of the Portuguese princess's dowry.

Despite the great territorial losses to the Dutch sustained by the Portuguese, it is striking how, in those lost areas, the lingua-franca has been a Portuguese-patois, while the Dutch tongue has totally disappeared from those areas they had once controlled. This language survival of the, generally, vanquished was due to the unceasing devotion of the Catholic missionaries. These were mainly members of the religious teaching orders, Franciscans, Dominicans and, above all, the Jesuits.

The subject of this account, however, is not the royal Portuguese empire as a whole but the history of one massive fortress they built upon the eastern coast of Africa at Mombasa, in modern Kenya (Map 1).

The Portuguese, when they first rounded the southern end of Africa and sailed northwards along its eastern flank, found upon its coasts there a well-developed civilisation, mainly an amalgam of Moslem Arabs and African women. As an area, it could compare, in its degree of civilisation, with the Indian littoral on the far side of that Ocean. Its central part was known as the Swahili Coast and broadly covered the shores of the modern Republics of Tanzania and Kenya. The word 'Swahili', in its origins was Arabic, not African, and originally stood for 'coasts'. It is now used to denote not only a geographical area but also a language spoken widely in those areas.

It may, at this point, be best to list the Portuguese forts that were to grow up along the eastern coast of Africa, listing them from south to north. First, after rounding the Cape, came Sofala, the guardian over the trade in gold extracted from the inland areas along the Zambesi River (Map 1). Next came the principal fort on the east African coast, S Sebastian on Mozambique island. In the Mozambique area as a whole there were several lesser forts, such as S Lourenço on an island in Mozambique bay and (later) the Red Fort at Lourenço Marques. However, if Mozambique fort had fallen, so too would have all those others. There had been another fort at Kilwa, to the north of Mozambique, but it was later abandoned. To the north of that again, lay the subject of this account, Fort Jesus at Mombasa. This small number of forts is an accurate indication of the 'back-water' status of the eastern side of Africa in the Portuguese heartland empire round the Indian Ocean. By far the greatest concentration of Portuguese political power lay along the western coast of India, despite the inroads made by the Dutch upon its southern end where, in 1663, they captured the town of Cochin and took over the lucrative pepper trade.

After an unsuccessful Dutch blockade of Goa, the Portuguese overseas capital, the Dutch attack up the western coast of India receded.

However, their place as Portugal's principal foe was then taken by the Omani Arabs, who in 1650 captured the Portuguese-defended town of Muscat. Thereafter, the Omanis built up an efficient navy and, in 1668, crossed the Indian Ocean and sacked Diu. On the Indian mainland, the Portuguese were seriously assailed by the rising power of the Hindu Marathas, with their capital at Poona (Map 1), who in the 1700s came close to capturing Goa itself.

We have spoken much of 'forts'. Just what is a fort? It is certainly not a castle, for the latter were built wholly in stone, with high, comparatively thin walls and towers. However, during the 1400s gunpowder and cannon had been developed, which could smash such defences. So during the 1500s and thereafter a new type of defence was evolved – a thick earthwork encased in stone to give it permanent form. This was the 'artillery fort', whose method of construction would have been as follows, where building on a level site was concerned.

First, the ditch would have been dug in a square, say, 200 feet (61m) long, 50 feet (15m) wide and 20 feet (6m) deep. The earth would be thrown up on the 'island' in the centre to form a bank, say, 15 feet (4.5m) high along its edges. If the ditch were left dry, this created a 'sunk wall', in this case of 35 feet. That digging would give a section as in Figure 1.

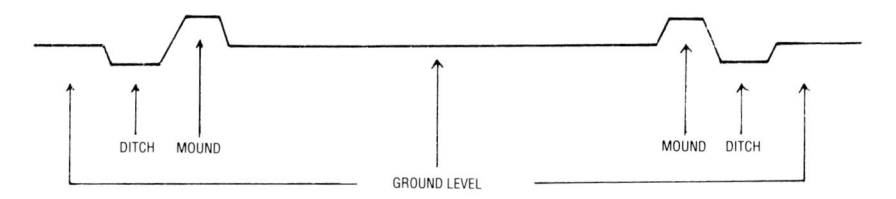

Figure 1 – Earthworks, section

The fort, however, was not meant merely to be passive. It was armed with cannon on its four-sided corner projections and was provided with thick earth and stone parapets over which musketeers could fire. The ditch would be crossed by a bridge, probably interrupted by a drawbridge, at the centre of one of its sides, to give a plan as in Figure 2. The gate would be arched for strength.

An essential part of an artillery fort from, say, about 1600 onwards was on the far side of the ditch. This was the glacis, a gently downward-sloping bank of earth, from the inner side of which was cut the covered-way, by which the garrison could pass unseen by an enemy without. The section of the completed works would then look like that shown in Figure 3.

The great merits of these thick, stone-encased earthworks were that the earth absorbed cannon balls and provided firm, wide platforms on which to operate its own cannon. Its demerits were that it was very costly to construct and that, as the system was refined, it spread itself outwards and so required an increasingly large and alert garrison.

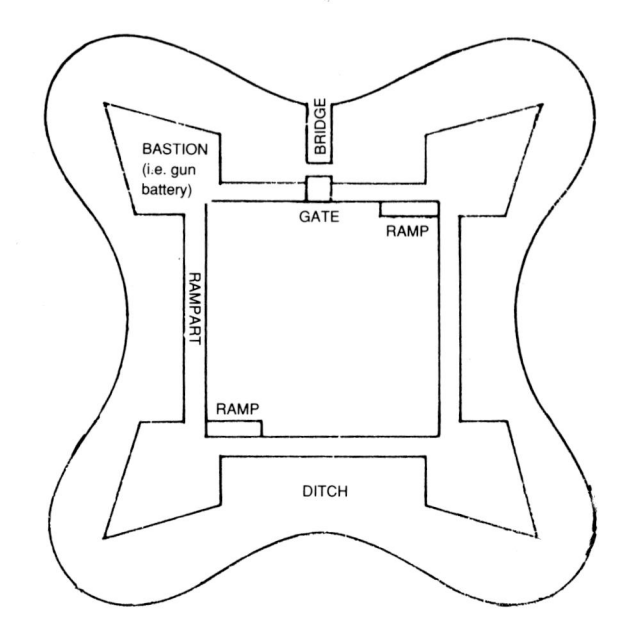

Figure 2 – Finished plan

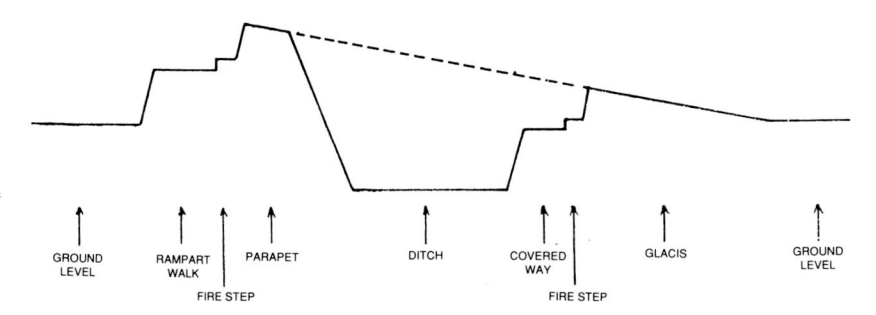

Figure 3 –Completed works, section

16

DESIGN AND HISTORY

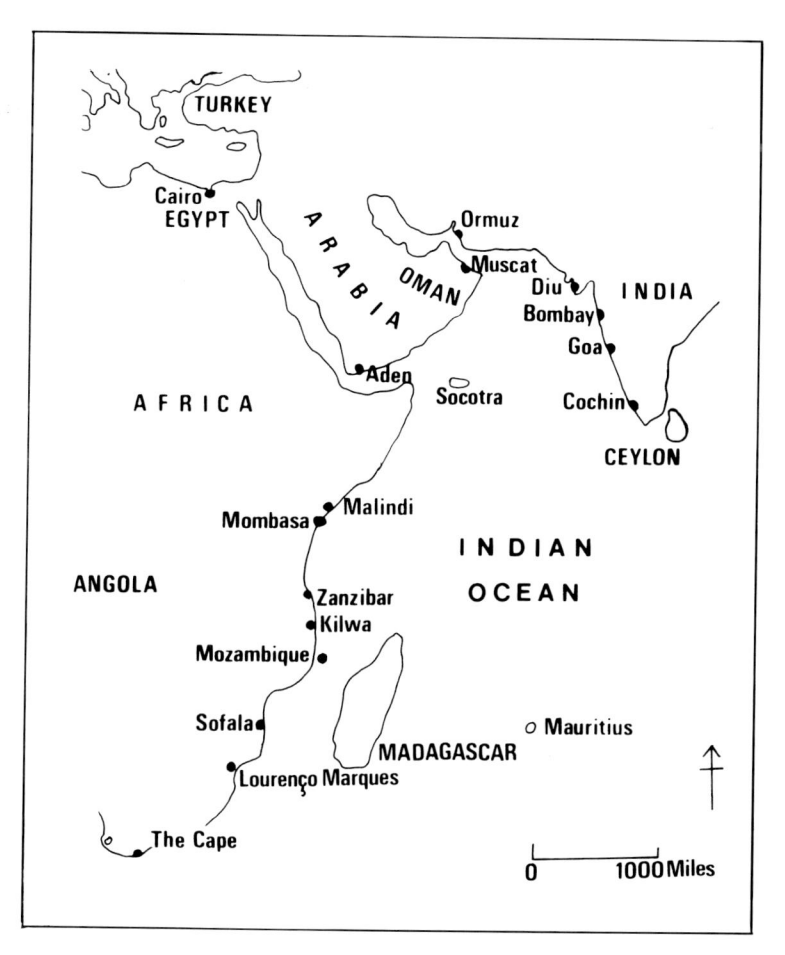

Map 2 – Eastern Africa, Oman and Persian Gulf

The above map of the entire eastern side of Africa, Arabian Oman and the entrance to the Persian Gulf, with the Indian Ocean to their east, is the setting in which lay Fort Jesus. It was really this stretch of sea and land that encapsulated the fort's all too bloodstained story. It also shows the area over which Portugal's influence, at one time paramount, was gradually whittled away by a number of more northerly rivals, of whom the Omani Arabs were to be the chief and the most damaging.

If the Portuguese physical presence on the Swahili Coast was so small, why did they go to the great trouble and expense of planting Fort Jesus upon it? The most important reason was the danger of the Turks coming down the Red Sea, which by the Portuguese failure to capture Aden in 1513 was an open avenue for enemy intrusions. Aden fell into the hands of the Turks in 1538. Thereafter, they were free to move southwards to capture, and then use as a base, Mombasa, which was by far the best natural harbour upon the coast. A Turkish sea captain, Mir Ali Bey, had already carried out this major raiding on two occasions in 1585 and 1588, on both of which – with the great advantage of his Moslem religion appealing to his fellow-Moslems – he had demolished the unfortified Portuguese mastery of the Swahili Coast as easily as one might blow over a house of cards. Admittedly, the second and larger raid had ended in disaster for him. A Portguese fleet from Goa crossed to Mombasa and caught him at anchor there. He was defeated and carried off as a captive to Goa. By forsaking his Moslem creed and becoming a Christian and by using tact and a natural skill in diplomacy, he did very well for himself. He was even used in positions of responsibility by his captors. As a result it might be thought that everything had ended for the best for everyone, but Mir Ali had given the Portuguese a major fright. He had demonstrated with painful clarity that, lacking any fortress upon the Swahili Coast and given their small physical presence there, the Christian Portuguese regime could be toppled at a push. The points of importance about Mombasa were that, not only was it the best harbour available but it was also an inveterate and bitter centre of Arab opposition to the Portuguese and was ideally placed for raiding the sailing route between Mozambique and the overseas capital at Goa on the west coast of India. Turks, once firmly established at Mombasa, upon the flank of the major sea route to India, could thus permanently threaten Portugal's empire lifeline. There was only one way to stop a repetition of Mir Ali's raids and that was to build a strong fortress at Mombasa and so both stultify the Arab resistance there and deny the Turks any future chance of securing this operational base in the Indian Ocean. This is why Mombasa possesses a fort that, for size and power, far exceeds the local needs.

Portugal, between the years 1580 and 1640, had fallen under the Spanish crown. Spain's King Philip II, although a difficult and imperious man, had a high sense of duty. He took in his stride the failure of the Armada against England in 1588 and turned his mind to more fundamental matters. These included questions of security in the east raised for his new Portuguese subjects by his becoming Philip I of Portugal. Within five years of the Armada, he was sending out to Mombasa one of his favourite military engineers, the Italian João Cairato, to found a new fort there. Cairato selected a site upon the end of a coral ridge that nearly reached the water, close to the antagonistic Arab town. Good as was the design in general, nevertheless it did contain one serious defect, the failure, in view of rising ground on two sides, to raise the top of the parapets much more than man-high above the level of the rock-top courtyard. Figure 4 shows how it was built originally and Figure 5 shows how it should have been done.

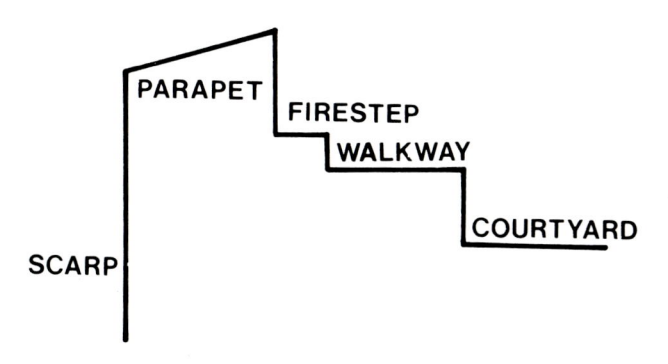

```
        ┌─┐
        │ │PARAPET
        │ │   ┌─┐
        │ │   │ │FIRESTEP
        │ │   │ └─┐
        │ │   │   │WALKWAY
        │ │   │   └──┐
        │ │   │      │
SCARP   │ │   │      │COURTYARD
        │ │   │      └────
        │ │
        │ │
        └─┘
```

Figure 4 – Parapets, as originally built

The first was undoubtedly cheaper but it led to centuries of not very effective tinkering by making additions to the parapet heights.

The outward appearance of the harbour front of Fort Jesus, as it stands today, is with its central gun platform thrust forward and, on each side, half-bastions sloped backwards, like birds' wings, to increase the field of fire over the entry passage into the old Mombasa harbour. The waters just in front of the Fort provide the safest passage through coral reefs, so passing ships could do no other than sail directly beneath its guns (Figure 6).

Mombasa island, which is some three miles (4.8 km.) long and two miles (3.2 km.) broad, was not given only the fort as a defensive protection. Two other sets of works, each consisting of three fortlets, were placed, first, on the cliff edge to the south of Fort Jesus to command the entry to Kilindini harbour that lay on the western side of the island and, second, at the Makupa ford at the north-west of the island, to guard against invasions by hostile and sometimes cannibal African tribes. All these six small forts have now vanished although their sites are known.

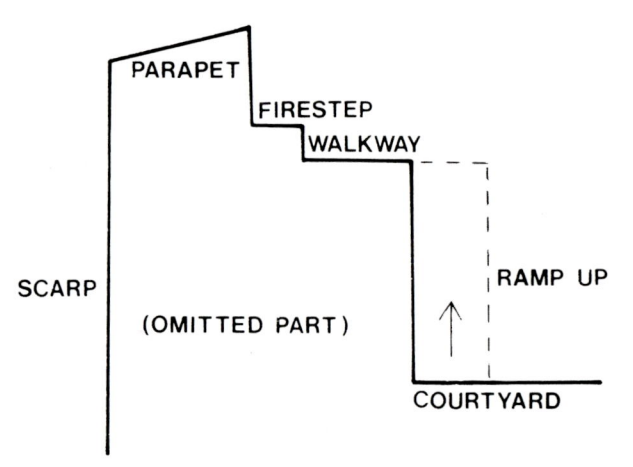

Figure 5 – Parapets that should have been built

Figure 6 – Fort Jesus, harbour front today

The stone inscription carved over the original outer gate of Fort Jesus recorded that it was founded in 1593, when Mateus Mendes de Vasconcelos arrived with the architect Cairato. He had with him Gaspar Rodriques, as Master of Works, whose duties were to see that the architect's plans were carried out exactly.

As well as the rocky coral ridge upon which stood the fort, the site has three additional advantages:

1 The low cliff and rocky shallows before it
2 The rocks and shoals in mid-channel, that forced vessels to sail close in to the Fort
3 The small sandy cove 100 yards (90 m.) to the south, that provided a supplementary landing place.

All these advantages gave the site, as a whole, great strengths. Had the ditch round its three landward sides been properly finished, it is probable that the Arabs would never have taken the fort, except by surprise, starvation or treachery.

The most important side of the fort was that which lay along the approaches to the harbour. So Cairato designed the fort with his main line of guns along that front and with the rest of the defences spread out backwards along the coral ridge.

The design he adopted was as shown in Plan 2.

The widespread non-completion before that date of parapets upon the tops of bastions and ramparts will be noted.

The fort's approximate measurements are 425 feet (130 m.) across the eastern harbour front, 425 feet (130 m.) from east to west (excluding the later-built outwork) and 325 feet (99 m) across the landward full bastions.

One crucial factor Cairato had to keep before him was the permanent shortage of Portuguese manpower. The fort's garrison would inevitably be small. In practice, it would seldom exceed half its complement of a little over a hundred men. So the place to be built would have to be one where such small numbers would suffice. The steep, rocky site he had chosen suited that requirement excellently.

He solved his problem by compromise. He adopted the bastion/rampart/ditch design but departed from the low, sloping profile which had the drawback of being more climbable and so calling for a larger garrison. Instead, he adopted high, vertical wallings, backed by solid rock (virtually indestructible) and plastered the exterior smooth to deny would-be climbers hand and footholds. It was really a very clever compromise.

Furthermore, as the fort was not only built round a rock core but also stood upon solid rock foundations, it was impervious to that great danger that could beset all fortifications, namely mining beneath the wallings to bring them down and so create a breach.

As has already been said, the harbour-fronting side of the fort was the most important and was provided with the most suitable and economic layout, that is, a central projecting rectangle, flanked by two backward-sloping half-bastions.

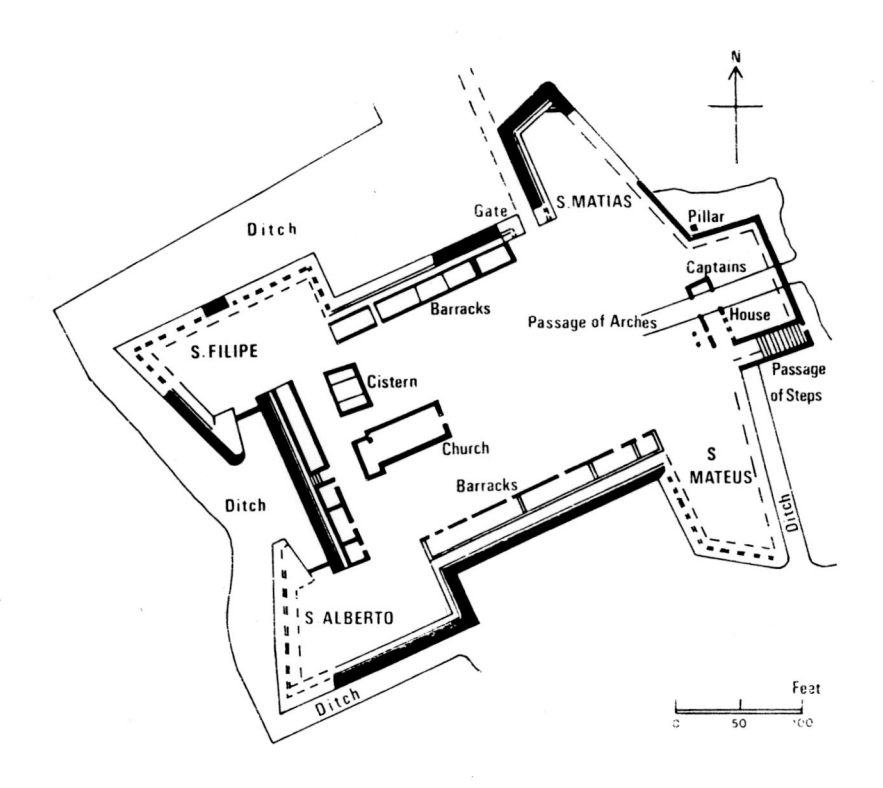

Plan 2 – Fort Jesus, *before* reconstruction was completed in 1635.
(Reproduced by kind permission of J. S. Kirkman)

Before dealing with the inward-lying parts of the fort, a word should be said on the saintly names by which are known the four major gun-platforms. These are:
1 Sea-facing Half-bastions
> S Mateus: named after Captain-Major Mateus Mendes de Vasconcelos, the officer-in-charge of the Portuguese fleet that brought Cairato to Mombasa; he became the first Captain of Mombasa.
> S Matias: named after Matias d'Albuquerque, who was Viceroy at Goa at the time of the founding of the fort.

2 Landward-facing full Bastions
> S Filipe: named after the King Philip II of Spain and I of Portugal,

who gave the order for the founding of the fort and sent Cairato to design it.

S Alberto: named after Archduke Albert of Hapsburg, Archbishop of Toledo and Viceroy of Portugal.

The four Half-bastions and Bastions were, therefore, named two after distinguished soldiers in the East and two after leading members of the Spanish royal family in Spain and Portugal.

Behind the sea-facing front lies the two-acre (0.8 ha.) central courtyard of the fort, with the entrance tucked in under the lee of the (later) S Matias elliptical extension.

Within the courtyard lay all the buildings that controlled Portuguese sovereignty over the Swahili Coast. Foremost among those was the residence and the offices of the Captains of Mombasa lying partly within and partly above the hollow rectangular projection. While this exposed position resulted in serious damage in time of siege, for day-to-day business control the high position was invaluable.

The courtyard contained also a building of a very different nature, namely the parish and/or garrison church, which was served by a visiting priest, who had a small house near it, close up against the main west rampart.

Along the north and south rampart parapets were lines of soldiers' barrack rooms. The foundations of the northern line still exist today.

Towards the west of the courtyard lay the garrison's lifeline, the water. This was a deep cistern filled by rain water channelled into it from nearby buildings. Just behind the cistern the Arabs, when they took the fort in 1698, made a deep well. This, unlike the rain-water cistern, was brackish.

At the extreme west end of the fort lie the two landward full bastions of S Filipe and S Alberto, each of which has two features not seen elsewhere; retired flanks and cavaliers, (that is raised gun-platforms) upon their salients. The purpose of the first was to protect the guns in the flanks from enemy counter battery fire. The purpose of the cavaliers was to increase fire-power, for S Filipe over the old Portuguese town and for S Alberto out towards the distant western harbour of Kilindini.

A visitor today sees the fort buried in the streets of a large modern city of over 300,000 inhabitants. The sentry who looked out over the fort walls when it was first built would have seen a very different scene of open countryside, with some half mile (0.8 k.) away the old hostile Arab town of Mombasa. Outside the fort's main gate lay the very small Portuguese town, which amounted to little more than a single street, called the Raposeira or Foxhole. Here lived the few Portuguese residents of Mombasa.

The dry ditch that surrounds the greater part of three sides of the fort is, in many ways, one of its most important and yet one of its most defective features, for it was never properly finished. The main weakness of the ditch is that, at its two eastern ends, it opens out and at those points leaves a comparatively easy approach to the fort walling. The weakness is compounded by an additional weakness at the southeast end of the ditch, where the walling is lower than elsewhere. The uncompleted ditch was dug with great slowness, despite urgings from the King at Lisbon and his Viceroy at Goa. It was cut, somewhat roughly and unevenly, out of the coral rock immediately surrounding the fort. On its inner side has been left a sloped coral base to the vertical wallings. On the outer side of the ditch, the bare coral has been left just as it had been cut, with no masonry counterscarp built against it.

Of the two peterings-out of the ditch, that at the north-eastern end was much the less serious, since the gate was well covered by three gun embrasures in the east flank of S Filipe, two being for large cannon and one for a smaller gun of the swivel type. It was at the opposite southeastern end that the serious flaw arose. There the ditch widened into open ground, wholly exposing the S Mateus salient to direct assault.

Before the founding of Fort Jesus in 1593 to counter the threat of Turkish eruptions into the Indian Ocean from the Red Sea, the Portuguese northern headquarters had been an unfortified factory at Malindi, whose Sultan was their sole Muslim ally upon the Swahili Coast. Their chief official there had been the 'Captain of the Coast', whose only armed support had been a small fleet of quite minor vessels.

From 1593 to 1631, that is during the first thirty-eight years of its existence, the fort had no history of strife or bloodshed. Then in 1631 came its first bloodbath.

The story of Sultan Yusif contains all the elements of Shakesperian tragedy, with the basically decent man going wrong, trapped into betraying either his Moslem faith or his Christian Portuguese allies. It led to an obscure and ignominious death as a wandering pirate, hunted by everyone.

The father of Muhammid Yusif had been the Moslem Sultan of Mombasa and had been murdered in 1614 by the African tribe of the Musengulos at the prompting of the then Captain of Mombasa. His son was taken to Goa and brought up as a Christian under the name of Dom Jeronimo Chingulia. In 1625, the Portuguese made him the Christian Sultan of Mombasa. The relationship between the new Sultan and the Captain of Mombasa rapidly worsened, until in 1631 came the explosion. The now Christian Sultan was seen by an informer secretly praying under cover of the darkness of night by the Moslem rites at the grave of his murdered Moslem father. The informer told the Captain of the Sultan's betrayal of his new Christian religion. The Sultan promptly had the informer murdered and decided to save his own life by reverting to his original Moslem faith and striking first. Gathering a band of Moslem followers, to whom he had imparted his design, he entered the fort (as he had a right to do, as he might have been coming to talk business with the Captain). He made his way to the gatehouse and there stabbed the Captain to death, while his followers spread through the fort killing all the Portuguese they could find. Over the next two weeks, all the Portuguese in Mombasa, men, women and children were slain by the rampaging Arabs and their African supporters. The numbers were surprisingly small, a mere 150, which confirms the small presence of the Portuguese on the Swahili Coast. However, even after beating off a punitive expedition from Goa, Yusif was unable to gain the respect of his new Moslem co-religionists and so, on 16 May 1632, the despairing Yusif abandoned Fort Jesus and sailed away in an armed ship to become a homeless pirate, who died at Jiddah six years later after a fight with fellow Moslems in the Red Sea.

The fort did not stand empty for long after the Sultan's flight. On 5 August 1632, it was re-occupied by the Portuguese. They at once set about strengthening it, to prevent any repetition of the Sultan's seizure. The improvements may be summed up as:

1 Strengthening the main gate, by adding a new outer gate, with a protective ellipse projection
2 Increasing the cannon fire-power over the harbour entrance, by adding an extra gun-platform to the seaward face of S Mateus Half-bastion
3 Adding gun-embrasures to the flanks of S Mateus Half-bastion and S Filipe Bastion
4 Adding to the cannon and musketry fire-power on the seaward side by building two angle towers at the junctions of the rectangular projection with the two Half-bastions.
5 Strengthening the defence of the rectangular projection by adding an outwork in front of it.

Plan 3 shows the fort, after the carrying out of these proposals.

By comparing this plan with Plan 2 one can see the improvements at once. They were completed, with speed and drive, by 1635.

The cavaliers on top of the two landward full Bastions were constructed as a pair by the Portuguese in 1648.

Apart from some later Arab additions and the Gulbenkian Foundation's new buildings, this is very largely the fort as we see it today (see Plan 1).

The military systems of the Portuguese on land and at sea during

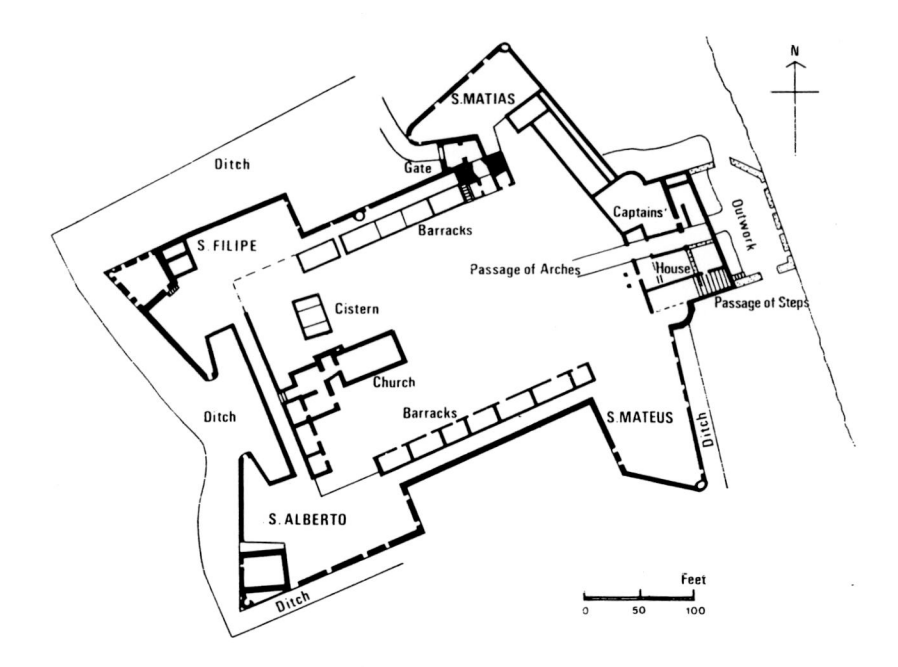

Plan 3 – Fort Jesus, *after* reconstruction by 1635 (Reproduced by kind permission of J. S. Kirkman)

the centuries of their empire deserve a word. First, they were very brave. But also it must be said that, all too often, they could be rash, ill-disciplined and badly-led. Many of their land defeats were self-made, since they held that honour demanded a headlong charge in all circumstances, no matter how unsuitable. A further weakness was the reliance they had to place on local levies (so often unreliable), to supplement their always inadequate numbers. Nevertheless, despite all these defects, on land the Portuguese always remained dangerous, since one never knew what they were going to do next. At sea, on the other hand, they very soon lost command to the far better organised and drilled Dutch fleets, so that those opponents early acquired the ability to move freely round the oceans, to transport troops as they willed and to blockade Portuguese ports as they chose.

So far, we have traced the development and history of Fort Jesus up to the reconstructions of 1635, plus the cavaliers added in 1648. Thereafter, the Portuguese were to hold it for only another fifty years. Even during those last years, the re-vitalised Arabs from the Sultanate of Oman at the eastern end of the Arabian Peninsula were pressing down upon them more and more. In 1660 the Omanis attacked and burned the Portuguese town of Mombasa, though they did not seek to assail the fort.

The fatal year was to be 1696. Then, a fleet bearing 1500 Arabs, mainly from Oman and the Swahili town of Pate, landed its troops on Mombasa island and establishd a base at Kilindini harbour. From there, they blockaded the fort from both the town and the open countryside of the island. Now the final test had come. On 13 March 1696 the Great Siege began. This was destined to last for just a few months short of three years and was to show, on the Portuguese side, acts of courage, loyalties, endurance and resolution, offset, alas, by cases of incompetence, irresolution and self-interest. On the Arab side, there was no marked inclination to close and force the issue. Their lack of really effective gun-power forced them back on to unglamorous blockade, with the ultimate hope of spreading disease and starvation and so forcing surrender.

The siege fell into three almost equal annual sessions, of which the first two were, in effect, ended by the arrival of small relief fleets from Goa. Tragically, the first annual relief also brought the plague. A more fatal accidental import could not have been conceived, for it meant, as actually happened, that one day the Arabs would enter the fort to find a mortuary, with next to no living garrison within it. The final disaster was made all the more certain by the incompetence and irresolution of the commanders of the relief fleets, who, after landing men and supplies, sailed off to Zanzibar and allowed the Arabs to reform their siege.

The defenders of the fort were an extraordinary and unlikely mixture. When the siege commenced, there were not above seventy Portuguese within the walls but they were aided by a substantial body of Swahili Moslems who, for whatever motives, preferred the Christian Portuguese to their own co-religionists from Oman. Most extraordinary of all, these Swahili contained a large number of women, who proved themselves to be excellent soldiers in the service of their religion's foes. The leading Swahili was Prince Daud of Faza (see Map 1). At one stage during the second year, when all the Portuguese had died, the Prince resolutely refused all Arab offers of favourable terms. It is good to know that he was safely evacuated by the second relief fleet.

That same second relief fleet also safely carried away the survivors of the many Mombasa Swahili civilians who had crowded for safety and shelter into the ditch at the start of the siege and had there endured horrible sufferings of dirt, disease and death.

In the close on three-year siege, the Arabs tried direct assault on only two occasions. The first was by daylight in July 1697 during the second annual period. This attempt to scale the walls was a total failure, the Arabs being repulsed with eighty men dead. The second Arab assault by night on 12 to 13 December 1698 was successful. The Arabs had learned from a captured boy that the garrison were dead from disease except for less than a dozen. So they mounted, at two points, the vulnerable salient of S Mateus Half-bastion and swarmed into the fort.

The nine surviving Portuguese and Swahili, under the Captain of Mombasa, Leonardo Soutomaior, retired to the top of the cavalier on S Filipe Bastion. There, they held out until seven o'clock the next morning. Then, after the death of the Captain, they surrendered. Fort Jesus had indeed at last fallen.

However, one final act remained, an act of courage and defiance. While the Arabs scattered all over the fort, hunting in every corner for the treasure it was supposed to contain but did not, one of the very few surviving Portuguese prisoners, a man named Antonio de Barboso, offered to lead his captors to the 'treasure' if they would spare his life. He led them to the gatehouse and took them into the powder-magazine on its first floor. There he contrived to explode the powder and so removed, at a single stroke, the whole top of the gatehouse, himself and a substantial number of gold-hungry Arabs. How he set off the powder is not known, since there were no survivors.

The siege cost the Portuguese 900–1000 men, plus an unknown number of their Swahili supporters. These losses were mainly from disease. They also lost a frigate, which sank just off the fort. Some of its timbers have been raised and now form an interesting exhibit in the Museum. The Arab losses would have been lower, since they were not closely confined or subject to the fatal diseases that ravaged the besieged.

The fall of Fort Jesus was indeed the end of Portuguese rule in Mombasa, apart from a brief and somewhat inglorious recovery of the fort in 1728–29. It also marked the total elimination of Portuguese power on the entire Swahili Coast.

The remaining Portuguese position around the Indian Ocean was, however, successfully maintained until the middle of the present century, when Goa, Daman and Diu were lost to India and Mozambique became an independent African state. This was a considerable feat for the Portuguese to achieve, although it must be said that the Omani Arabs at Mombasa from 1698 were not so serious a threat to the Portuguese Indian Ocean position as had been the eruption of the Turks from the Red Sea in 1585 and 1588.

The story of Fort Jesus while it was in Arab hands between 1698 and 1895, when the British took it over in the founding of the new Protectorate of East Africa, was one of decline and of dissensions between the various Arab powers in Oman and along the Swahili Coast. The fort fell into some decay and dereliction. The courtyard became filled with shacks and occasional dilapidated houses. The Arab garrison was sometimes non-existent or was down to one or two caretakers. Repairs were not kept up-to-date or were often carelessly done. Worst of all, the fort was allowed to fall into near-obsolescence over the period of some 200 years of Arab occupation by failure to add outworks beyond the ditch or other fortification improvements. This had allowed advancing gunnery and explosives to put the fort half out-of-date.

One permanent and unresolved difficulty over the effective control of the fort was the chronic rivalry for its possession between the Sultans of Oman, the Mazrui Sultans of Mombasa and the Sultans of Zanzibar.

Of those inter-Arab disputings, one of the most bloodstained occurred in 1747, when the Sultan of Oman sent assassins to murder the Mazrui Sultan of Mombasa. In this, they succeeded but they failed to catch his brother, who, with reinforcements, forced his way back into the fort and executed the assassins.

As the end of the 1800s approached, it was the Zanzibar rulers who had succeeded in controlling the fort. In 1875, at their Sultan's request in order to subdue a rebellious governor, two British warships bombarded the fort and quickly brought about its surrender. The fort was now having to pay for two centuries of military neglect, for it had no up-to-date guns with which to oppose the warships.

This bombardment was the cloud upon the horizon; the precursor of things to come. Colonial European eyes were upon East Africa and British and German fleets in 1895 moved in upon the unfortunate Sultan of Zanzibar. He could not resist the threat posed by modern warships. He had no option but to surrender and to withdraw to his island and others near it and to give up both the Swahili Coast and mainland Africa to the colonial powers. Thus, in 1895, British East African Protectorate (in 1920 renamed Kenya) and German Tanganika came into existence and Arab rule upon the Swahili Coast came to an end.

A DESCRIPTION

THE EXTERIOR

As there are advantages, when examining a fort for the first time, in doing so from its exterior, that will be done for Fort Jesus, starting at the sole remaining gateway, which lies on its northern side. There, the dry ditch, as it approaches the sea edge of the fort, widens out into a shallow depression between the Bastion of S Filipe (on the right in Figure 7) and the elliptical extension of the Half-bastion of S Matias at the left in Figure 7.

Figure 7 – Northern Entry

One of the minor but confusing difficulties in describing the two Half-bastions of S Matias and S Mateus is the wholly accidental similarity of their names.

Close to S Matias, a stone-built causeway crosses the depression at a

Figure 8 – S Filipe recessed flank

rising angle of approach, to disappear behind the extension on the left, where the fort's main gate lies. At the moment nothing more will be said about the gate, as it will be described more fully later. Instead, a move will be made to the right. Along the centre lies the straight line of the main north rampart with, on the right, one flank and part of one face of the S Filipe Bastion. In the flank can be clearly seen two large arched gun embrasures covering the gate opposite (see Plan 1).

While heights vary along this northern front, the general figure is some 50 feet (15 m). It is vertical and covered with smooth plaster. It is more or less unclimbable, and would be when under fire.

Further to the right, is the ditch along the western side of the fort, where lie the two landward facing full-Bastions of S Filipe and S Alberto.

In many ways, the recessed southern flank of S Filipe (seen above) and the corresponding recessed northern flank of S Alberto, taken in combination, make the most impressive and daunting defences of the

Figure 9 – S Alberto, west face and ditch

fort. Figure 8 shows clearly two points of interest on the coral base upon which the Fort stands.
1 The uncovered grey rock
2 The inward slope of that base

The recessing of flanks was intended, among other purposes, to provide sheltered positions for cannon flanking adjoining ramparts and bastions. In this case, however, the provision of cannon within both recessed flanks can only be described as slight. They were saved from failing in their purpose only by the reasonably adequate provision of musketry loopholes.

The west face of S Alberto runs up to that Bastion's salient, where the ditch turns along the fort's southern front. Gun embrasures of the salient cavalier and a stone sentry box can be seen on the upper left and centre of Figure 9. Although they cannot be made out from the photograph, a panel containing the arms of the Archduke Albert of Hapsburg is on the right hand edge of S Alberto Bastion.

On the extreme right of Figure 9 there are some low caves in the counterscarp.

The ditch now turns off leftwards along the south side of the fort.

On the left of Figure 10, is the eastern flank of S Alberto, with one open-topped gun embrasure looking up towards S Mateus Half-bastion's west flank and south face. In the angle between the Bastion and the fort's main south rampart are:

1 A coral-built Arab sentry box
2 The foundations of an Arab-built curved latrine tower, which had been entered from beside the sentry box.

Figure 10 – S Alberto and latrine tower foundations

Figure 11 – East end of south ditch

A word should be said on the patched and frequently discoloured plasterwork. Not only were repairs frequently carried out to the plaster over the centuries but also the tropical sun has had its effects upon it.

Figure 11 clearly demonstrates the one real flaw in the fort's defences; the fading out of the southern ditch at a point where the fort's walling was, in any case, lower than the usual height. The ditch here becomes open ground with rising land behind it. The whole extent of S Mateus Half-bastion lies open to direct and unimpeded assault. The ill-effects of this ditch 'fade-out' could have been quite simply adjusted by digging a deep and wide supplementary ditch in the rock immediately below S Mateus on the right above. However, nobody ever did it.

To the right of the preceding photograph (Figure 11), lies the eastern, harbour-facing face of S Mateus, across which the Portuguese had dug a shallow and inadequate ditch. At the extreme left of the walling (Figure 12) can just be seen the arms of Mateus de Vasconcelos with, above them, the top of a stone sentry-box at the Half-bastion's salient. Clearly seen also are three of the five arched gun-embrasures added after the Sultan's rising. Between them are musketry loops, usually two to three between each pair. The low height of the walling is here very apparent. Its reason was the fall-away in the ground level as one moved northwards along the harbour front. The Portuguese could not help that fall-away but they might have partially overcome its

Figure 12 – S Mateus, postern and coral cutting

draw-back by adding also a gun-cavalier upon the salient of the Half-bastion.

In the centre of Figure 12 there are two interesting features:
1 The square plaster patch marking the exit from the now blocked postern gate in S Mateus
2 A cutting down the steep coral slope to provide an additional side exit to the harbour waters.

Before the central projecting rectangle lies a low outwork intended to provide a covering entrance to the fort from the small sandy cove a hundred yards (90 m.) to the south and also additional gunfire over the harbour entrance.

Figure 13 shows one of the outwork gun-embrasures with a cannon barrel lying within it. The single-sailed vessel seen through the outer

Figure 13 – Outwork gun embrasure

arch illustrates perfectly the closeness to the fort's guns forced upon shipping by the mid-channel coral reefs.

In Figure 14 Fort Jesus is shown as it appears on the many postcards which so impress the visitors from the numerous holiday hotels.

In the foreground is the northern exterior of the low outwork, from its cliff-edge on the left across to its junction with the rectangular projection towards the right. The latter looks at its best from this angle, with its height, its colour, its Arab battlements and sentry-box.

Figure 15 is partly the same view on the left but has added to it on the right the northern angle tower and the length of S Matias east face, with before them the open esplanade which was once guarded by a defendable wall along its harbour edge.

This east face of S Matias Half-bastion merits a view on its own (Figure 16). Lacking explosive shells or aerial bombs, one could do little with it. Internally, it is one solid rock core. It is 50 feet (15 m) high,

Figure 14 – Outwork and rectangular projection

Figure 15 – Outwork, projection. North angle tower and S Matias east face

vertical and smooth and a very different proposition to its flawed fellow Half-bastion.

Figure 16 – S Matias, east face

Above the centre of the parapet, the Kenyan flag, which flies from the gate ellipse, can just be seen. Its tiny size stresses the height of this Half-bastion's face.

This completes the circuit of the exterior of the fort and brings us back to the entrance gateway, just round the Half-bastion salient on the right above.

THE ENTRANCE

The curve of the rising causeway (uninterrupted by any drawbridge) is shown in Figure 17. It circles the ellipse before the gate. Over the gate is a stone inscription recording the completion of the improvements made to the fort after the Sultan's rising.

THE COURTYARD

Through the main outer gate, along an outer covered tunnel, then, after a right-angled turn, and passing through an inner gate (now marked by an open-work iron grille), followed by an arched entry passage, takes a visitor into the large two-acre (0.8 ha.) central courtyard of the fort. This is now filled with many buildings, both ancient and modern, and also with the foundations of very many other old buildings.

The whole fort was most generously restored by the Gulbenkian

Figure 17 – Outer gate, from depression

Figure 18 – Church foundations, end-on, and view across courtyard

Foundation of Lisbon round about the year 1960 to the state in which it had been in Portuguese and Arab days, a restoration that also removed almost all traces of the intervening British period when the fort was used as a prison. The various structures within the courtyard should be listed. They are

Old	New
Gatehouse	Museum
Church	Former Curator's house (now offices)
Clergy house	
Cistern	Ticket office
Well	Toilets
Barracks	Under construction
Two Arab houses	Refreshment room
Captains' house	New shop
Mazrui house	Car parking is outside the fort in the north ditch
Guard room	

In addition:
  Four Bastions or Half-bastions
  Three ramparts
  Three passages (blocked)
  Rectangular projection
  Outwork
  Cannon and ammunition

Figure 18 shows the courtyard looking across it from the western rampart parapet interior to the distant buildings in the background. In the foreground, are the foundations of the small parish or garrison church, as seen from one end. Concealed behind the trees on the far left lies the gatehouse, with the pinkish coloured Arab Mazuri house in the right background and with the end of the new Museum on the extreme right.

The trees and grass within the courtyard are made possible by the shallow earth covering, that now lies upon much of the coral core of the fort.

Here, in Figure 19, the unintended camouflaging effects of the mottled grey and brownish plaster intrude. This, lying close to the church remains, is the still intact, though now dry, large cistern which supplied the Portuguese with all their water needs in the fort, although it frequently leaked and the water was often impure. It is 56 ft (17 m) deep. When it was in use, it was filled by rainwater channelled into it by pipes and drains. It was built by the Portuguese in 1603. The new Museum can be seen over the top of it.

Figure 19 – Cistern, rear view

Figure 20 – Museum and guns

So far, things examined have all been either Portuguese or Arab. Yet much of the life of the fort has been spent under the British or the Kenyan governments.

The British proclaimed a Protectorate over the East African coast from 1 July 1895 and turned the fort into a prison. Little trace now remains of the prison occupation. By and large, it was all swept away at the restoration from 1958.

By far the most prominent part of those restorations is the new Museum, which was set up along the line of the south barrack block, where previously prison cells had stood. This is an admirable example of how a Museum should be laid out. It contains not only a very wide range of finds discovered within the fort but also numerous Arab exhibits which have been brought in.

Fort Jesus contains a remarkable number of cannon, or rather cannon barrels, totalling close on seventy. Only one is now mounted on a proper wheeled carriage, the rest lying on concrete or wooden blocks or upon the ground. The best preserved barrels are the twenty which are shown in Figure 20 outside the Museum (Appendix A sets out the cannon and cannon ammunition situations more fully).

A less well-preserved set of barrels is lined up on the ground near the main north rampart (Figure 21).

Many are corroded and some are broken. Near them lies a pile of iron cannon balls of various calibres, together with a few stone balls.

This end view of the house (Figure 22) of the Arab Mazrui Sultans of Mombasa is not very impressive. The house itself is small, the red

Figure 21 – Gun barrels and ammunition, by north rampart

Figure 22 – Mazrui house, end view

plaster is patchy, the coconut frond roof is not neat and the various floors are of decreasing width. The front and rear views are more impressive but they are not very photogenic. Yet the Mazrui dynasty ruled Mombasa from here for close on a century, although they are also reported to have lived in a house in the town.

Between the Mazrui house and the shattered remnant of the Captains' house lie the commencements of the two underground routes down to the outwork. The larger and more important is the Passage of the Arches (Figure 23) and the lesser is the Passage of the Steps (both so called because the sloped first had arches across it to bear the Captains' house and the second because it consisted of steps).

The bright light is the tropical sun shining through the spaces between the three arches which had borne the weight of the Captains' house. The very steep, roughly hewn slope leads down to the blocked exit into the outwork. On the right, can be seen three steps that lead into two ammunition stores, opening one off the other. These stores are

Figure 23 – Passage of the Arches, arches and slope

cut out of the solid coral rock. They were very damp when first found by the restorers.

Not far from the inner entrance of the gatehouse, there is a very fine example of an Arab door set in a wall (Figure 24).

It opens down the middle, the centre post swinging. It is laminated for strength, with three layers of wood, as in three-ply boarding. The carved decoration is profuse and, being Islamic, is of geometrical patterns only. It is studded with rows of brass spikes. Two bolts, operated from the inside, secure the leaves in place. Texts from the Koran appear over it, although here the shadow obscures them.

Figure 24 – Arab door, by ticket office

THE RAMPART PARAPETS AND BASTION PLATFORMS

It might now be appropriate to leave the courtyard as such, and to consider one or two aspects of the ramparts, the four Bastions and Half-bastions and the eastern rectangular projection; all as seen from their courtyard sides.

First, the rectangular projection shows the most obvious and eye-catching of the upper works added to the tops of wallings. These are the added Arab battlements (Figure 25).

It is an extraordinary sight, where one row of Arab battlements has been placed straight on top of a lower row, with the junction clearly

Figure 25 – Rectangular projection, Arab battlements on its south side

visible. Indeed, the small embrasures between the merlons of the lower row have been left open to act as musketry loopholes in the heightened walling. The irregular shapes of the pointed merlons will be noted. A

Figure 26 – Main north rampart and barracks

large square gun-embrasure looks out, flanking the east face of S Mateus. The thinness of the walling can be seen at the gun-embrasure's edge. Presumably, the purpose of the upper addition was to screen from view rather than to give substantial protection. The visibility of the Captains' and Mazrui houses may have been the reason for the addition.

In Figure 26 we have a comprehensive view of the interior of the main north rampart. In the centre distance is the tall oblong gatehouse, with on its left-hand ground floor the former outer gate to the fort (now converted into the inner gate by the addition of the elliptical extension of the west flank of S Matias Half-bastion and the construction of a new outer gate in the lee of the extension). On the near side of the gatehouse is a second-floor doorway and a flight of exterior steps leading down to a kitchen and a lavatory. In the near centre is the modern white toilet, the only restoration structure that does not quite fit into its

Figure 27 – Main south rampart, parapet interior

surroundings. In the right distance is the reddish ticket office. The centre foreground is occupied by the foundations of the soldiers' north barrack block. To the rear of them are the parapet walkway and the interior of the parapet itself. Against that parapet stands a two-tier stone sentry-box, of which the lower part is Portuguese and the upper Arab work. This box overlooked the outer main gate, the old Portuguese town and, in the distance, the Sultan's palace.

If a move is now made to the interior of the opposite, that is the south, rampart parapet, a clear example will be seen (Figure 27) of the heightenings carried out, over the centuries, of the original too low Portuguese parapets. Down the centre runs the original walkway. To its immediate right is the stone firestep, with, again to its right, the original Portuguese parapet itself, running across the lower right centre.

Figure 28 – S Mateus, gun platform musketry loophole

Then, along the upper right and centre, are the two rows of heightening added to the outer downward-sloping edge of the original parapet, the upper and later addition being the thinner.

The building along the left is the rear of the new Museum.

In the distance in the far left centre, the east parapet of S Mateus Half-bastion is just visible.

The interior of an Arab musketry loophole is shown in Figure 28. It is interspersed between the gun-embrasures on S Mateus gun platform. This demonstrates the form – pointed, recessed and with a smoke-escape hole above it.

On the grass outside the fort stand two guns of a very different nature (Figure 29). They are two naval guns, which, after having been salvaged from the water, are now mounted on wheels for land service.

According to the notice standing between them, they were part of the main armament of eight such guns of the small British light cruiser *Pegasus*, which was sunk in 1914 in the opening weeks of the First World War by the somewhat heavier German light cruiser *Koenigsberg* of very similar armament. *Pegasus* had had to go into Zanzibar harbour to the south of Mombasa for repairs to her boilers. While there, she was caught by the unexpected appearance of her larger rival and was sunk at anchor. However, *Koenigsberg* was herself sunk in somewhat similar circumstances some months later, after a long blockade up the shallow

Figure 29 – Two naval 4" guns from the First World War

Rifuji River, still further to the south of Zanzibar island. To achieve this, two shallow-draught monitors were brought out to East Africa. In the second of two long-range gunnery duels, they successfuly sank *Koenigsberg* at her moorings.

Despite the statement on the notice board, it is possible that one of these two guns came, not from *Pegasus*, but from *Koenigsberg*. It will be noted from the photograph that the two barrels are dissimilar, which would be unlikely in the main armament of a warship.

CONCLUSION

Fort Jesus has had much to tell of itself over the centuries from 1593 as well as of its turbulent relationships with the complex populations upon the narrow coastal strip along the Indian Ocean's western fringe; of its equally turbulent relationships with the shifting black races that appeared and disappeared from the high inland plateaux of the vastnesses of mainland Africa and of the trading, on the monsoon winds, all around the Indian Ocean. It had also clearly succeeded in the primary object of its founding, effectively to exclude the Turks from establishing a base in East Africa.

There are many functions to be carried out by any fort but, ultimately, it has to be judged by military standards, that is to say, on its ability to withstand successfully attacks made upon it and on its providing a safe and secure base from which foes may be assaulted. It is, therefore, upon those military assessments that Fort Jesus should be judged. That judgment should take account of time and place when, from East Africa, it took six months by sail for a query to reach Europe via the Portuguese Viceroy at Goa and a year for a reply to be received by the same roundabout route.

The military assessment would be based on:
1 The soundness of the building design in the light of military theory and practice at the time of its building
2 The fort's history of assaults sustained and of attacks launched from it
3 The extent to which, over the centuries of its military life, it developed and adapted to meet successfully the improvements in both
   (a) artillery and explosives and
   (b) the theory of assault by siegecraft and by improving engineering skills and methods.

In judging these points, proper regard will have to be given to the manner in which Fort Jesus has lasted, as good today as when it was built in 1593 or, rather, in its improved form of 1635. Yet that very longevity carries with it a major qualification. During that long period the military world had not been standing still. Very many improvements and developments in fortification had taken place to meet the ever-increasing power of explosives and of artillery. This applied, in particular, to defences on the far side of a fort's ditch, called, in general, 'outworks'.

As explosives have technically improved and have become more destructive, the ranges of artillery and of rockets have steadily and inexorably increased. To meet these improved ranges successfully, defences have had to spread themselves outwards further and further. In a fortress of the type of Fort Jesus, that is a single unit basically of four bastions, the first and most essential outward spread would be to cross the ditch and build additional fortifications on its far side. These quickly became of a standard pattern of three elements:
1 A 'covered way', which does not mean something under a roof but a means of passage sheltered from fire from outside
2 A 'glacis', which is a gently downward sloping bank of earth, free of all obstructions and shelter for an enemy, out of the inner side of which the covered way is cut
3 A 'ravelin', an advanced triangular gun and musketry platform, designed to sweep with its fire the adjoining glacis.

These outer defences were normally provided with additional ditches out beyond them. In other words, the whole fortress became larger, more difficult to control from surprise or localised attacks and requiring an increasingly larger and more active garrison. Ultimately, it also meant money, both to build the extensions and to man them. War was becoming more and more costly.

Figure 30 – Fort George, triangular ravelin, dry ditches, bridges and covered way (photograph by Scottish Development Department)

CONCLUSION

Fort Jesus has had much to tell of itself over the centuries from 1593 as well as of its turbulent relationships with the complex populations upon the narrow coastal strip along the Indian Ocean's western fringe; of its equally turbulent relationships with the shifting black races that appeared and disappeared from the high inland plateaux of the vastnesses of mainland Africa and of the trading, on the monsoon winds, all around the Indian Ocean. It had also clearly succeeded in the primary object of its founding, effectively to exclude the Turks from establishing a base in East Africa.

There are many functions to be carried out by any fort but, ultimately, it has to be judged by military standards, that is to say, on its ability to withstand successfully attacks made upon it and on its providing a safe and secure base from which foes may be assaulted. It is, therefore, upon those military assessments that Fort Jesus should be judged. That judgment should take account of time and place when, from East Africa, it took six months by sail for a query to reach Europe via the Portuguese Viceroy at Goa and a year for a reply to be received by the same roundabout route.

The military assessment would be based on:
1 The soundness of the building design in the light of military theory and practice at the time of its building
2 The fort's history of assaults sustained and of attacks launched from it
3 The extent to which, over the centuries of its military life, it developed and adapted to meet successfully the improvements in both
   (a) artillery and explosives and
   (b) the theory of assault by siegecraft and by improving engineering skills and methods.

In judging these points, proper regard will have to be given to the manner in which Fort Jesus has lasted, as good today as when it was built in 1593 or, rather, in its improved form of 1635. Yet that very longevity carries with it a major qualification. During that long period the military world had not been standing still. Very many improvements and developments in fortification had taken place to meet the ever-increasing power of explosives and of artillery. This applied, in particular, to defences on the far side of a fort's ditch, called, in general, 'outworks'.

As explosives have technically improved and have become more destructive, the ranges of artillery and of rockets have steadily and inexorably increased. To meet these improved ranges successfully, defences have had to spread themselves outwards further and further. In a fortress of the type of Fort Jesus, that is a single unit basically of four bastions, the first and most essential outward spread would be to cross the ditch and build additional fortifications on its far side. These quickly became of a standard pattern of three elements:

1 A 'covered way', which does not mean something under a roof but a means of passage sheltered from fire from outside
2 A 'glacis', which is a gently downward sloping bank of earth, free of all obstructions and shelter for an enemy, out of the inner side of which the covered way is cut
3 A 'ravelin', an advanced triangular gun and musketry platform, designed to sweep with its fire the adjoining glacis.

These outer defences were normally provided with additional ditches out beyond them. In other words, the whole fortress became larger, more difficult to control from surprise or localised attacks and requiring an increasingly larger and more active garrison. Ultimately, it also meant money, both to build the extensions and to man them. War was becoming more and more costly.

Figure 30 – Fort George, triangular ravelin, dry ditches, bridges and covered way (photograph by Scottish Development Department)

A good example of such outworks beyond the main fort ditch is provided by the very large Fort George built during the second half of the 1700s on a peninsula upon the shore of the Moray Firth in northern Scotland to control the rebellious Highlanders and to deny to the French fleet a chance to attack the Highland capital of Inverness higher up that Firth.

Those huge outer works show clearly how far Fort Jesus had been left behind in military technical advances during the years covered by the 1700s. However, time and place must again be remembered. It needed the national finances of Spain and Britain to build Fort Jesus and Fort George. The Portuguese and the Arabs who later held Fort Jesus did not have a fraction of the money required to introduce up-to-date improvements and developments.

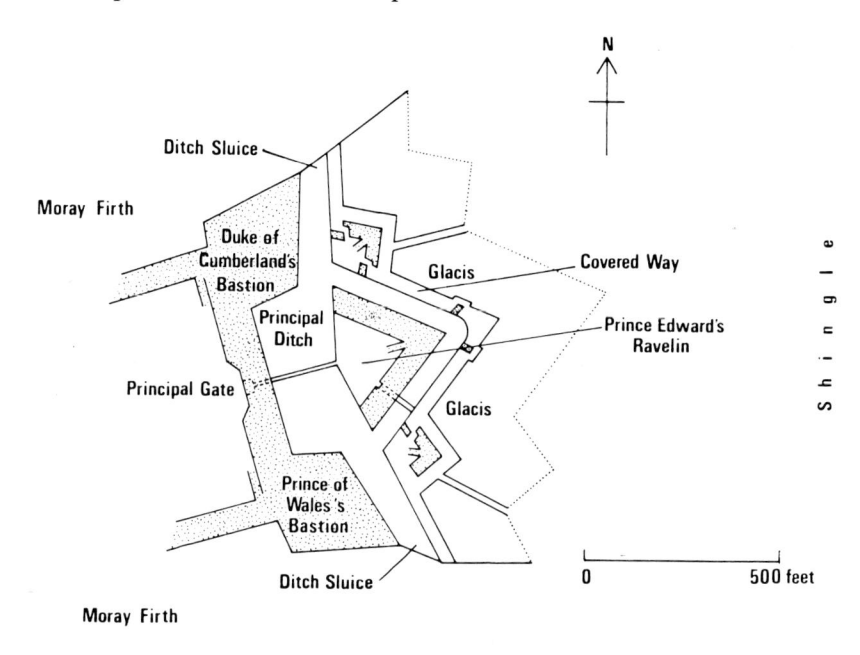

Plan 4 – Fort George, outworks, principal ditch and east bastions; yet another fort lying east-north-east by west-south-west (plan by Scottish Development Department)

The ravelin in the photograph appears in the centre of the plan. It has before it a supplementary ditch with, beyond that, a covered way with two strong points upon it and then a sloping glacis. Beyond that again, lie extensive areas of shingle that would have made the digging of attackers' siegeworks very difficult. By the mid-1700s date, the ravelin had become a major piece of fortification. It will be seen that at Fort George it is as large as either of the bastions in its rear.

At Fort Jesus nothing at all was ever built on the far side of the ditch. For that, there were a number of reasons:
1 The Portuguese had never been able to spare more than a handful of men to hold it or the East African coast in general; they were under constant and increasing pressure in northern and western India from the Omanis, the Marathas and the English. Fort Jesus had to take its chance as best it could
2 The Arabs, after they had captured it in 1698, were principally engaged in wars with each other and, as none of them had really effective artillery, the old fortifications continued to be adequate, if patched up as they went along
3 Nobody had the kind of money fortification improvements required.

Then, as the centuries passed, even the foregoing form of close-in outworks ceased to serve, as artillery power increased. So the system of defence by a continuous line of works was broken up into rings of separate forts covering each other by cross-fire.

As none of these developments had taken place at Fort Jesus, the old walls and the old ditch continued to serve until 1875 when the Fort was assailed by the rifled guns and the rockets of a European naval Power. Then the wrinkles showed.

On the basis of that military assessment, what is the verdict on Fort Jesus? That verdict might be summed up, as follows:
1 On balance, it is favourable, despite its lack of extension developments and its ultimate falling out of date; that favourable verdict arises, more than anything else, because of its combined massive coral core and its height; those assets would usually leave an attacker little prospect of successful assault and would drive him back on to the far slower blockade, with its ultimate starvation and disease.
Note: Many 'impregnable' castles, such as Harlech in North Wales, succumbed to blockade; shut in for eight months, it surrendered in 1409 after horrible sufferings by the beleaguered garrison from starvation and disease, to which in Harlech's case were added thirst and intense winter cold; most of Harlech's garrison were dead when it finally surrendered, with the few survivors mere half-living skeletons.
2 That verdict is, in fact, confirmed by the nature of the fort's fall in 1698 to the Omanis; one Arab assault had been decisively repulsed and the besiegers had had to fall back upon a continuance of the slow blockade, until the garrison was as good as wiped out by plague.
3 If the 'favourable on balance' verdict is considered in the light of the three military assessments, it will be seen that it passes the first

(soundness of design) and the second (history of assaults and sallies) but fails the third (extensions and adaptations to meet new forms of assault). However, that third has to be seen, not in general terms, but in the circumstances pertaining for centuries upon the long narrow seafaring Arab-dominated strip of the low-lying Swahili Coast. It was the one and only strong place for hundreds of miles north and south of itself. Inland lay the savage, wild, unpenetrated plateau of mainland Africa, inhabited by uncertain tribes, sometimes cannibal, who appeared and disappeared in a totally unpredictable manner, often hostile or at the best potentially so. The Portuguese seldom numbered more than, say, fifty men in Mombasa capable of bearing arms, so numbers were certain to be overwhelmingly against them when they faced the Omanis; their requirement, therefore, was not for a fully up-to-date fortress but one in which the numerous Arabs could not reach them, that is to say, the 50 foot (15 m) high Fort Jesus. So it might not unfairly be said that, in those circumstances, the third assessment was not, for Fort Jesus, of particular relevance.

The many friends of the fort can, therefore, still be assured that it passes all reasonable standards of judgment and can permanently rank as Kenya's splendid foremost historical monument.

Fort Jesus is also exceptional in that, by reason of its absence of later developments and its most careful restorations, it stands today in its late medieval form and has been spared the demolitions that have overtaken so many other fortifications all over the world. Such intact survivals are sometimes called time capsules.

However, the fort has always been something more than just a fortress. It has always been a part of the Arab civilisation coastline of eastern Africa. So now a brief glance will be taken outside its walls up to its historic ally at Malindi, lying some 70 miles (113 km.) to Mombasa's north.

MALINDI AND GEDI

Some historians have referred to the period of European colonial expansions as the 'Vasco da Gama era'. That tough old Portuguese sailor might have been surprised if he had known that he would provide the label. However, surprised or not, he appears in Mombasa just outside Fort Jesus, in the old Portuguese town, in Vasco da Gama Street.

Figure 31 – Vasco da Gama Street, Mombasa

Here, the old houses on both sides are interrupted by a white Arab building (Figure 31). The absence of litter is as striking as it was in and around Fort Jesus.

Here, shutters, balconies and overhanging roof eaves are very noticeable in the older houses.

By no means are all Mombasa streets old and narrow. This fruit

Figure 32 – Fruit market, Mombasa

Figure 33 – Moslem mosque, Mombasa

57

selling is taking place (Figure 32) in a wide modern thoroughfare. The racial mixture is both interesting and instructive. Once again, no litter. The fine quality of the fruit is also striking.

The Moslem faith brought southwards over many centuries of steady Arab colonisation along the East African coast is clearly demonstrated by this fine Mombasa mosque (Figure 33). Islam is now the predominant religious faith along the coast, although there are also many Christians, Hindus and Sikhs.

The coastal road running north crosses a river by a car ferry at Kilifi. There are many large houses and many expensive-looking yachts, belonging to the thriving local yacht club. The area is clearly prosperous.

Figure 34 – Kenyan seashore

Much of the coast road runs past beach or sea scenes, such as shown in Figure 34, before it reaches Malindi. Across the centre, out to sea, is the white line where the waves break upon the coral reef.

Malindi, despite its comparatively small size, achieved fame and importance during the Portuguese period (say, AD 1500–1700) by being, among all the Arab settlements, Portugal's sole Moslem ally.

From the first exploratory voyage in 1498 up the eastern side of Africa by Da Gama, Malindi alone welcomed him as a friend. This was, in part at least, because of Malindi's long-standing enmity towards the Arab town of Mombasa. The latter, incidentally, had been particularly hostile to Da Gama when he had first appeared in his ships off their port. Malindi and the Portuguese were, therefore, to some extent, thrown together by their common dislike of Mombasa.

As a mark of recognition for their loyalty to the Christian Portuguese crown, the King of Portugal gave Da Gama a white stone pillar, surmounted by the arms of Portugal, to present to the Sultan of Malindi. On his second voyage to India, Da Gama again called at Malindi and gave the, possibly secretly embarrassed, Sultan his awkward gift. Then he sailed on to India, leaving the Sultan feeling a little conspicious all alone with his well-meant pillar. So, what with one thing and another, the pillar remained discreetly unerected.

Then Da Gama re-appeared and the fur flew. Hastily, the pillar was taken out of its seclusion and erected upon the rocky shore of Malindi. The Sultan must have felt some sympathy with tightrope-walkers. He lived in constant alarm at his larger and more powerful Arab neighbours, who regarded him as a traitor to his race and his Moslem religion. But the more urgent and immediate danger was the irate Da Gama, who was on the spot, afloat with his guns run out off his town.

Figure 35 – Da Gama pillar at Malindi

So, with the Sultan's affable smiles but nervous looks over the shoulder, up went the pillar.

The Sultan need not, in fact, have worried, for quite shortly afterwards, the Portuguese sacked Mombasa and broke its power.

Figure 35 shows the pillar upon Malindi's shore. The arms of Portugal, fortunately, have just cleared the clouds. Seated at its base is Kassim, a very knowledgeable taxi driver who took the writer twice a day between the hotel and the fort. The circular 'collar' round the pillar's base was added in the late 1800s to keep it stable.

A few miles south of Malindi, splendidly excavated by Dr J. S. Kirkman from the engulfing jungle, lie the remains of the walled and gated Arab town of Gedi. The buildings are of interest to this account of Fort Jesus, because the whole civilisation of the Swahili Coast was Arab/African and because the fort itself fell to the Arabs in 1698. Fort Jesus cannot be considered as just a Portuguese stronghold. It is part of an Arabised community and buildings erected by Arabs properly pertain to the fort and the fort to them.

Figure 36 – Gedi, the Palace gate

The remains of Gedi cover a wide area and are reached by trim, well-kept paths through the silent jungle. The exhibits include a specially arranged and inhabited small village to demonstrate the way of life when Gedi was itself inhabited.

The central point of interest is the remains of the Sultan's Palace, with an arched gateway, recessed back into a squared and decorated framework (Figure 36).

Figure 37 – Gedi, house gateway

Figure 38 – Gedi, house remains and well

A more simple form of gateway gave entry to a house (Figure 37).

These house remains (Figure 38) have three arched doorways, again set in squared frames within walls of small stonework. In the foreground is a circular well, now covered by an iron grille.

Figure 39 – Gedi, pillar tomb

Tombs with tall pillars erected over them are especially interesting, being partly Arab and partly African. They are found mainly in East Africa and in Ethiopia. Both the pillar and the tomb beneath it shown in Figure 39 are decorated in Arab geometrical patterns.

Figure 40 – Gedi, tree splitting and supporting length of walling

Some 400 years ago, this wall surrounded a prosperous Arab town. Now, its traders and settlers have all gone and no more than a fragment of wall, split and held up by a tree, remains to show its past. Thus does nature overtake the works of man.

APPENDIX A

FORT JESUS of Mombasa: CANNON AND CANNON BALLS

1 Fort Jesus possesses, around its various areas, an astonishingly high number of cannon of various calibres and weights of shot, together with a large supply of solid cannon balls (mainly of iron but some of stone) and a few hollow iron mortar bombs.

   The cannon are principally Royal Navy rejects given to friendly rulers at Fort Jesus when they had become obsolete for use in European naval wars. Most of those so donated were given during the 1700s and 1800s.

2 The total held, including a number which are by now much corroded by rust or have been broken (mainly at the muzzle ends and that possibly by the action of salt sea water) number no less than sixty-six. This is an accumulation far in excess of the Fort's normal artillery armament at any one time in the past. That would not have been likely to have exceeded something in the order of twenty pieces. Even at the latter figure, it would almost certainly have been substantially higher than any likely foe (except, at one time, possibly the Dutch) would have been able to bring into action. Not until the bombardment by the Royal Navy in 1875, when explosive shell was successfully used against the fort, was surrender forced upon it by gunfire.

3 A most comprehensive survey of all cannon and cannon ammunition in his book *Fort Jesus, A Portuguese Fortress on the East African Coast* was made by Dr Kirkman in 1974 to a total of fifty-nine pieces of ordnance. These are summarised on pages 152–4 of the book and might be stated as being:

(a) **Ordnance**

Material of make	Weight of shot	Country of origin	Century of Manufacture	Number of Guns
Iron	4 lbs	England	1800s	1
	6 lbs	England	1600–1700s	6
	18 lbs	England	1700–1800s	30
	24 lbs	England	1700–1800s	10
	Carronades	England	1800s	6
	42 lbs	England	1700s	1
	24 lbs	France	1700s	1
	18 lbs	Sweden	1700s	1
	32 lbs	Venice	1600s	1
Brass	6 lbs	England	1800s	2
			Total Guns	59

The carronade was invented at Carron in Scotland in the later years of the 1700s. It was a short gun, 4.5 feet (1.4 m) long and with a wide bore of approximately 6.75 inches (17 cm). It was widely used by the Royal Navy, although it received some set-backs in single-ship defeats by American frigates in the British-American War of 1812. It was often used as a bow-gun and frequently against enemy crews, when it would be loaded with case or grape, which were both multiple small shot containers which produced a 'shrapnel' type of effect.

The average lengths and bores of the most common of the iron English cannon at Fort Jesus are:
18 pounders – 6.5 ft (2 m), 5 ins (13 cm) bore
24 pounders – 7.5-8 ft (2.25–2.5 m), 5.5-6 ins (14–15.25 cm) bore.

4 Where cannon and carronades have been referred to, it should strictly-speaking be to gun barrels for, with one exception, none of them is mounted on a proper four-wheeled wooden carriage. The latter will have perished or been broken up.

Instead they stand now on wooden blocks, stones or pieces of concrete. Some lie upon the ground. The one exception is a 24 lb cannon in the elliptical gate projection, where it stands in a gun-embrasure overlooking the main street of the old Portuguese town.

5 The guns at the present day which alone are in perfect condition are the two brass six pounders. Brass or bronze guns had many advantages over iron guns (steel, as we know it today, had not then been developed). The chief advantages were that they did not rust and that they were stronger and less brittle than iron guns and so could be made lighter. They were less likely to burst on firing (the most celebrated fatal casualty from an iron gun burst was King James II of Scotland, standing too close to a gun, when it was fired at the siege of Roxburgh Castle in 1460). The drawbacks to brass or bronze guns were that the material was harder to work and so required a higher degree of skill and that there were shortages of the copper and zinc needed for making brass and of the copper and tin required for making bronze. The really over-riding disadvantage was the higher cost of manufacture. On the other hand, iron ore was plentiful and comparatively easy to work. So brass and bronze guns became a luxury and the cheaper, weaker and heavier iron guns became almost the rule. There is an economists' theory that the less good drives out the better.

6 Today, the gun barrels that stand in and outside Fort Jesus are, in general, not laid out in order of shot weights, countries of origin or gun conditions. There might conceivably be room for re-consideration of such points, particularly as at present it is not easy to identify all individual guns. The existing locations of the guns are:

Outside the Museum	20
Outside the north barrack rooms	11
On S Filipe cavalier	1
On S Mateus Bastion	2
Near the ticket office	5

On the rectangular east projection	4
In the elliptical gate projection	2
In the outwork	4
By the First World War Memorial	6
Outside and around the main gate	5
On the football pitch at the sea edge	6
Total guns	66

It will be noted that the sixty-six detailed above exceeds Dr Kirkman's figure of fifty-nine by seven. There may have been additional acquisitions since his book was published in 1974 or the fifty-nine may not have included certain guns in an advanced condition of decay or seriously damaged.

7 Far and away the guns in the best condition are the twenty lined up outside the Museum. The eighteen iron guns there are free from rust and the two brass barrels are perfect. There is extremely useful and informative detail on these guns appended near them. This might perhaps with advantage be extended and possibly a guided tour of all the guns in the fort might be included in the visitors' itineraries. If such an inclusion were being considered, there might be a case for restoring some of the missing gun-carriages, perhaps as a start with some of the twenty barrels outside the Museum.

8 A point that is particularly relevant is that so great a collection of smoothbore solid shot cannon all in one place must be very unusual. In this aspect also, Fort Jesus stands alone upon the East African coast.

(b) **Cannon ammunition**

Dr Kirkman, on his pages 154–5, summarises the cannon ammunition found within the fort, as follows:

Iron

In ammunition store off the Passage of the Arches	
– solid	2,255
– hollow	3
In other areas	
– solid	404
– hollow	47
	2,709
Stone	
In ammunition store	–
In other areas	54
	2,763

At the present time, the ammunition store is empty and large piles of shot lie was follows:

Three by the north barrack block

One in the corner by S Filipe cavalier

In addition, many cannon balls are at present receiving treatment in the maintenance workshop beneath the former Curator's house. On the cavalier of S Alberto, lie two mortar bombs, one of which is broken.

APPENDIX B

FORT JESUS of Mombasa: GUN-EMBRASURES AND LOOPHOLES

1 At first sight, the fort does not seem to be particularly well provided with arrangements by which fire could be brought to bear upon an enemy outside the walls. There is an almost total absence, both of gun-embrasures and of loopholes (except in the low outwork) anywhere other than at parapet level. Although the number of, in particular, loopholes at that level is large, the openings-defence gives an impression of being 'all higgeldy-piggeldy', that is, of being distributed in disorderly fashion and thus leaving the possiblity of blind spots at the foot of the walls.
2 However, a careful examination of wall openings indicates that this is not so and that, with the major proviso that the garrison would have to be both alert and of adequate numbers, a safe approach to the fort for the purpose of escalade would be extremely difficult to achieve and would be costly in casualties.
3 In the matter of wall defence-openings, it must be stressed that the fort, during its active days, had been occupied by a succession of powers, Portuguese, Arab and British, all of whom had their own political priorities and all of whom adapted the fortifications to suit their particular purposes.
4 All the defensive wall-openings, both gun-embrasures and loopholes, have been counted, circling round the courtyard anti-clockwise from S Mateus, via S Matias, S Filipe and S Alberto and thence back to S Mateus. All openings were included, whether they were large or small gun-embrasures and whether the loopholes were large and carefully shaped or were just rectangular spaces left open. The counts were as overleaf:

(a) **Gun-embrasures**

Location	Total	Bastions	Projection	Ramparts & Outwork
S Mateus	8	8		
South Angle tower	1		1	
Rectangular projection	6		6	
North Angle tower	1		1	
S Matias	2	2		
Ellipse	2	2		
North rampart	2			2
S Filipe	14	14		
West rampart	2			2
S Alberto	12	12		
South rampart	5 (blocked)			5
Outwork	4		4	
	59	38	12	9

(b) **Loopholes**

Location	Total	Bastions	Projection	Ramparts & Outwork
S Mateus	25	25		
South Angle tower	–		–	
Rectangular projection	47		47	
North Angle tower	2		2	
S Matias	34	34		
Ellipse	8	8		
North rampart	17			17
S Filipe	29	29		
West rampart	16			16
S Alberto	30	30		
South rampart	42			42
Outwork	10		10	
	260	126	59	75

At fifty-nine and two hundred and sixty, these totals are large but the following points need to be kept in mind:

Gun-embrasures – the figures for S Filipe (fourteen) and S Alberto (twelve) include embrasures on the cavaliers, while S Mateus (eight) includes those on the added gun platform.

Loopholes – a very high proportion of these are in the heightened added wallings on top of the original artillery parapets; some are not conveniently placed and would be hard to work from efficiently.

APPENDIX C

FORT JESUS of Mombasa: STONE SENTRY BOXES OR WATCHTOWERS

1 Fort Jesus possesses, built upon bastion salients or at selected strategic points, nine coral stone sentry boxes or watchtowers. These were built in either the Portuguese or the Arab periods, six and a half belonging to the latter.
2 As look-outs, they were not particularly effective, as they were not corbelled out beyond the features upon which they stood but were set back slightly within them, so that their fields of view were partially obscured by masonry beneath them. Neither are their observation openings large or numerous. They are small squares or rectangles placed low down and numbering only two or three for each sentry box. Possibly, as most of these were built by the Arabs, the low positioning would not have mattered greatly, since Arabs often seat themselves on rugs or cushions.

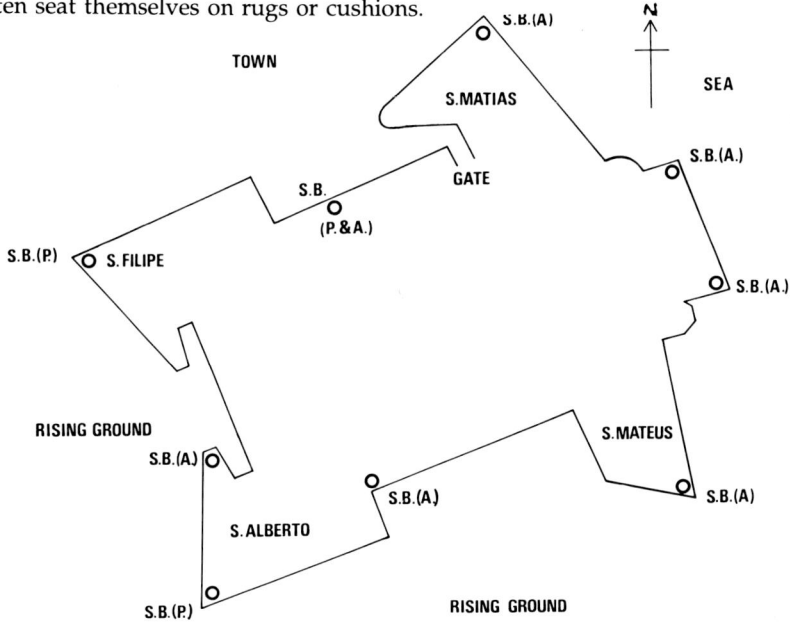

SENTRY BOXES – O S.B.
PORTUGUESE – (P.)
ARAB – (A.)

Plan 5 – Positions of sentry boxes

3 Most of the sentry boxes are reached by short flights of two or three steps. All are either arched or have square-headed lintels and have cupola-shaped roofs. They are also all capped by various designs of ornaments.
4 Only one is two-tiered, the lower half being Portuguese; the upper half is Arab. This double sentry box lies on the main north rampart, comparatively close to the outer gate, which it overlooks. Its extra height enables it also to overlook the approach from the old Portuguese town and, in the distance, the Palace of the Sultans of Mombasa.
5 The positioning of the sentry boxes is as shown in Plan 5.

By and large, the Portuguese had dispensed with stone-built sentry-boxes, except on the later two western cavaliers and in the lower half of that on the north rampart. It was the Arabs who later, at various dates, added the rest. Four of them were upon salients on the harbour-facing east front. The remaining two and a half, however, were directed landwards. The half was a special heightening to look over the town to the north. Another, on the south, overlooked the Arabs' point of entry into S Mateus salient in 1698. The purpose of the last, that at the point of S Alberto's retired flank is not clear. In practice, it blocked off a gun-embrasure and crowded out effective defence of the flank's point.

APPENDIX D

FORT JESUS of Mombasa: ARTILLERY FORTIFICATION TERMS

Note: Arranged not alphabetically but in sequence from bastion to beyond the ditch.

Bastion: a four-sided work which projects from the main rampart, often at the corners; it consists of two long straight faces and two short flanks; the latter may be straight or may be recessed.
Note: A half-bastion has only three sides, two long and one short; as one short side is, for good practical reasons, omitted, flanking fire is not provided along one of its ramparts.

Rampart: a thick, inwards-sloping wall, which forms the main defence of a fortress; it is made of earth and is most often wholly or partly encased in stone at front and back; it is provided with a thick parapet along its outer side.
Note: The stretch of rampart running between two bastions may also be called a curtain.

Parapet: a thick earth protection (usually wholly or partly encased in stone), along the outer edges of bastions and ramparts to shield the garrison; provided with embrasures and firesteps.

Embrasure: an opening cut through a parapet, from which cannon were fired; usually made narrow on the inside and splayed wider on the outside.

Firestep: most usually one row (but might be two or three rows, one above the other) of steps along the foot of a parapet for standing on when firing over its top; when not on a firestep, a man would be concealed from outside by the height of the parapet.

Salient: the point at which the two longer faces of a bastion meet, often at under a right-angle though sometimes at over the ninety degrees.

Face: the name given to the longer side of a bastion, as it faces towards the open country, into which it is given a field of fire free of obstructions.

Flank: the name given to the shorter side of a bastion, which usually meets its adjoining rampart at a right angle; it serves to give flanking fire along that rampart and also to the face of the adjoining bastion; sometimes it is recessed, to give additional protection to the guns within it.

Ditch: a wide, deep trench, sometimes filled with water, sometimes left dry, separating the bastions and curtains from the ground outside. In fortifications with works on the far side of the ditch, dry ditches were sometimes preferred as routes by which the garrison could move quickly and unseen from one point to another; crossed by a bridge, often provided with a drawbridge.

Drawbridge: the later, lighter, carefully balanced and more easily worked form was operated by just two men, by counterpoise like a pair of scales; pivoted overhead beams were attached to the far side of a moveable hinged section of the bridge and were heavily weighted at the inner end, usually by stones. By pulling the weighted end down by hanging ropes, the whole could be swung up and over in a matter of seconds; the raised section of bridge then protected the gate; could also be used in the middle of a bridge, divorced from stonework.
Note: Fort Jesus is not provided with any drawbridges.
Scarp: the exterior stone casing covering the earth core of a bastion or rampart; usually sloped inwards as it rises to meet the exterior of the parapet.
Counterscarp: the stone walling on the far side of the ditch, lining the earth usually down to the foot of the ditch.
Covered way: a wide walk on the far side of the ditch, open to the sky, cut out of the inner edges of the glacis: supplied with a musketry firestep; soldiers upon a covered way were protected from the enemy's view when not upon the firestep.
Glacis: a wide, open, gentle slope of earth on the far side of the ditch, intended to concceal the lower part of the main fortifications and to provide a free field of fire; perhaps six to seven feet high on the inside and sloping down to ground level at its outside edge.
Ravelin: outer cannon battery on the far side of the ditch, to support the musketry fire from the covered way and to give flanking fire over the glacis, from which it is usually separated by its own smaller ditch; triangular-shaped with open base (gorge) facing the inner rampart, so as to give no cover to an intruding enemy; connected to the curtain by a causeway, sometimes broken by a drawbridge, across a wet ditch or reached by steps from a dry one.
Note: Fort Jesus developed no works at the far side of the ditch.

APPENDIX E

THE FORT OF S SEBASTIAN at Mozambique

(Based on J. S. Kirkman's *Men and Monuments* and the Plan and photographs reproduced with his kind permission)

1 If the true place of Fort Jesus in the Indian Ocean and in the world-wide Portuguese empire is to be fully understood, it is essential to relate that massive outpost on Mombasa island to its sister fortress of S Sebastian on Mozambique island, 1000 miles to its south. This is so because:
   a) S Sebastian, which was founded in 1558 to the design of the noted Portuguese military architect and engineer Miguel de Arruda, was by far the larger of the two and lay at the heart of an area much more thickly populated with Portuguese citizens. Unlike Fort Jesus, which was the sole fortress in its area, Mozambique fort had round it several other strongholds. These included the triangular S Lourenço on an islet in Mozambique bay. On the mainland were the fort of Mossural at Cabeceira, another at Sofala, one in the Kerimba islands to the north and, at Lourenço Marques, the Red Fort.
   b) the only route to and from Europe lay round the Cape and the fort at Mozambique was, therefore, an essential link between Lisbon and the Portuguese overseas capital at Goa; if S Sebastian had been lost, the entire empire to its east could not have been sustained.
   c) the role of S Sebastian in the Portuguese empire as a whole was, therefore, far greater than was the more limited function of Fort Jesus to its north; the latter's role, though essential for holding the northern part of the East African coast, was more localised and thus more limited.
2 The plan of S Sebastian is given in Plan 6.
   At first glance, this looks an oddly designed place, with three of its four ramparts given an inwards bend at their centres, where wide obtuse angles are formed. Only the shortest of the ramparts, that between the Bastion of Nossa Senhora (Our Lady) and the Bastion of S Barbara is straight. There, the ground is level and open. The lines followed by the three other ramparts are, for the two sea-edge wallings, settled by the inward-curving shorelines and, for the single landward-facing walling, by the advantage of obliging an attacker upon the fort's main gate to, as it were, put his head into a bag in advancing between thrust-forward bastions upon a 'withdrawn' gate.
   The four bastions also have marked peculiarities. The two seaward

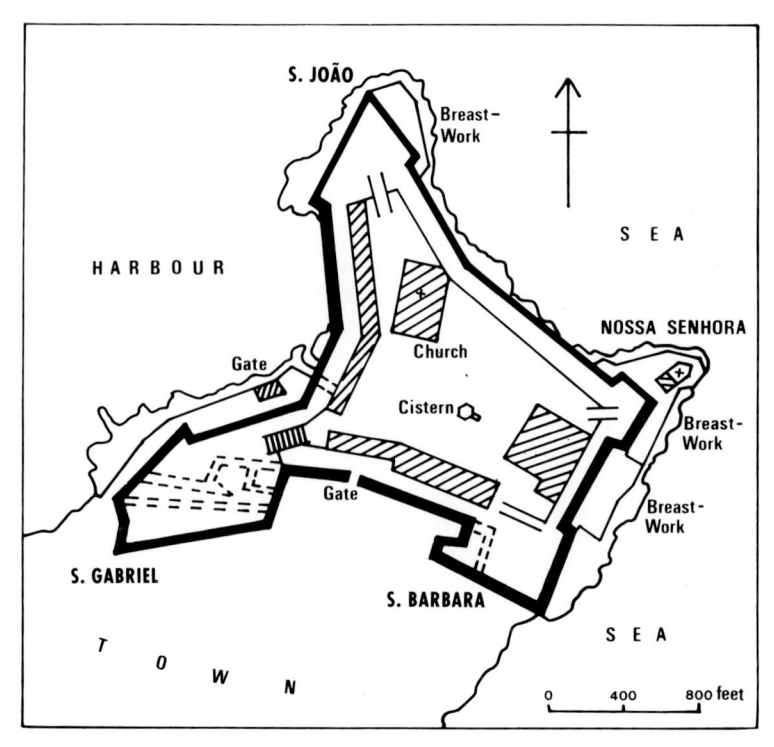

Plan 6 – S Sebastian, Mozambique

Bastions of S João and Nossa Senhora have extremely short flanks. So short are they that their power to enfilade effectively the adjoining ramparts must have been considerably reduced, partly through diminution in the number of guns available and, in the case of S João, by one flank lying at an obtuse angle to its adjoining rampart.

The short lengths of the flanks of those same two seaward Bastions caused them to be, in effect, triangular, instead of the normal four-sided figure.

The Bastion of S Barbara contains a preserved recessed square-cut flank similar to those on the two landward-facing Bastions of S Filipe and S Alberto at Fort Jesus. Both the Bastions of S Barbara and S Gabriel were, over the centuries, the subjects of constant re-building, indicating, with the years, various changes of mind. These changes are shown in Plan 6 by the dotted lines. Should there be recessed flanks or not? The result is a combination of both answers.

The dotted lines of S Barbara indicate a later leftward addition to the town side face, with inside it a new recessed flank. The more complicated dotted lines of S Gabriel indicate a successesion of, to some extent, changing ideas:
a) an original triangular-shaped Bastion, with a small three-sided recessed flank.

b) an outward extension of the townside face, in a straight line, with a recess of corresponding shape and position to that at present surviving in S Barbara.

c) a further outward extension towards the town of the above long face, with a curious inward bend in the walling lining the approach to the harbour gate; at some stage, the previously existing recess was filled in.

The succession of extensions to S Gabriel has made it into a very large Bastion of a most odd six-sided shape, designed apparently to give simultaneous maximum flanking with its guns to the approaches to the main gate and to the harbour gate. There may also possibly have been thoughts of overawing the town, either in civil disturbances or during occupation by an enemy. In Dr Kirkman's graphic expression, this Bastion came to resemble the giant claw of a hermit crab.

Figure 41 – S Sebastian, approach to harbour gate

3 The fort had originally had three gates:
   a) the main gate, facing the town and set back in the rampart between S Gabriel and S Barbara.
   b) the harbour gate, similarly set back in the rampart between S Gabriel and S João and
   c) a postern, now blocked, leading out into the breastwork outside the Bastion of Nossa Senhora; that breastwork was destroyed by the sea and the postern was then blocked and replaced by two others made to give into new breastworks built against the seaward sides of the Bastions of Nossa Senhora and S João.

The main gate was blocked by the garrison at the time of the first Dutch siege in 1607. It was regarded as too vulnerable to fire from cannon landed from the attackers' ships. The walling on the main gate side was also vulnerable to mining, as it was built on sand and was nearly brought down by the Dutch in their first siege in 1607. The main gate has only comparatively recently been re-opened. It had been replaced as the fort's principal gate by the harbour gate, which was hard to approach by land past S Gabriel Bastion and could not be bombarded very effectively from the harbour.

4 The Portuguese hero of the two unsuccessful sieges by the Dutch in 1607 and 1608 was the garrison commander, Dom Estevao de Ataide. It would have been well for him if he had died at that time or had left the East. Unhappily, he stayed on and fell into disgrace through mismanaging affairs in the Zambesi area. He died a pauper in the town of Mozambique in 1613, cared for by the Jesuits, whom he had previously befriended.

That town is nowadays a small Portuguese/African port, with many interesting old houses and churches. None of the houses, however, dates to before the burnings of the town by the Dutch and the Arabs duing the 1600s.

Figure 42 – S Sebastian, Our Lady of the Bulwark chapel

5 Outside the Bastions of S João, Nossa Senhora and near S Barbara lie some interesting outer defended areas along the sea edges. Breastworks occupy the shoreline promontories off the salients of the first two of these Bastions. That off Nosa Senhora is occupied by a small chapel, that of Our Lady of the Bulwark (Figure 42). As can be seen from the illustration here the chapel is whitewashed and has attractive steps and arches. The picture also shows detail of the breastwork walling height of six feet (1.8 m), parapet fire-steps of solid blocks of coral and open-topped cannon embrasures, firing out to sea off the Bastion salient, just showing on the left. This breastwork was clearly meant to be a practical fighting platform, despite the attractive chapel.

On a stretch of flat ground between the Bastions of Nossa Senhora and S Barbara and lying behind the protection of a continuation of the breastwork parapet round the chapel is an open area that used to serve as a place of execution and as a burial ground.

6 The five acres (2 ha) central courtyard of the fort is occupied by many buildings, which include a large chapel (which had a rather chequered history) and a cistern. There was no fresh water on the island and the garrison had to depend on the collection of rain in cisterns for a water supply. This system of water collection may well have been at the root of the severe malarial state of Mozambique, since mosquitos breed in stagnant water.

   Plan 6 indicates that ascent to the platforms of the Bastions of S João, Nossa Senhora and S Barbara was by sloped ramps, while there appear to be steps to the top of S Gabriel.
7 Dr Kirkman's photograph (Figure 41) of the approach to the harbour gate shows a surprisingly full complement of cannon in the open-topped embrasures of S Gabriel, S João and the rampart connecting them. Every embrasure is occupied by a cannon, at least those in the two Bastions being mounted on carriages. This is an impressive display.
8 That same photograph (Figure 41) seems to indicate the existence of a ditch before S Gabriel. All the works shown are of the standard 'artillery fortification' pattern, with moderate height, sloped scarps, rolled mouldings, upright parapets and open-topped embrasures. The great height, the plastered surfaces and (for many of the openings) the arched gun-embrasures of Fort Jesus do not occur here.

BIBLIOGRAPHY

(restricted to books held by the writer)

Aberdeen University Colloquium Proceedings, *Africa and the Sea*, (Aberdeen University African Studies Group, Aberdeen, 1985)

Boxer, C.R. and C. de Azevedo, *Fort Jesus and the Portuguese in Mombasa 1593–1729* (Hollis & Carter, London, 1960)

Boxer, C.R., *The Portuguese Seaborne Empire 1415–1825* (Hutchinson, London, 1969)

Cipolla, C.M., *Guns and sails in the Early European Expansion 1400–1700* (Collins, London, 1965)

Duffy, C., *Siege Warfare 1494–1660* (Routledge and Kegan Paul, London, 1979)

Duffy, C., *The Fortress in the Age of Vauban and Frederick the Great 1660–1789* (Routledge and Kegan Paul, London, 1985)

Kirkman, J.S., *Fort Jesus. A Portuguese Fortress on the East African Coast* (Clarendon Press, Oxford, 1974)

Kirkman, J.S., *Guide to Fort Jesus, Mombasa* (Kenya National Parks, Mombasa, 1960)

Kirkman, J.S., *Men and Monuments on the East African Coast* (Lutterworth, London, 1964)

Nelson, W.A., *The Dutch Forts of Sri Lanka* (Canongate, Edinburgh, 1984)

Padfield, P., *Guns at Sea* (Evelyn, London, 1973)

Strandes, J., *The Portuguese Period in East Africa* (East African Literature Bureau, translated from German by Jean F. Wallwork, Nairobi, 1961)

INDEX

A Mina 12
Aberdeen University 10
Abubakar, A. 10
Abyssinia 12
Aden 13,18
Africa 9, 11, 12, 13, 14, 17, 19, 24, 25, 28, 29, 51, 54, 55, 60, 62
Albuquerque, M. 22
Allen, J. 10
Ammunition stores 43
Angle towers 25, 36
Angola 13
Arab door 44
Arabian Peninsula 27
Arabs, 9, 12, 14, 15, 17–19, 21, 23, 25, 27–29, 33, 36, 40–42, 45, 48, 49, 53–56, 58–60, 62, 76
Archbishop of Toledo 23
Archduke Albert 23, 33
Arches 15, 36, 38, 43, 76, 77
Argium 12
Armada 18, 19
Arms 33, 34, 59, 60
Arrude, M. de 73
Artillery 51, 52, 54
Artillery fortification terms 71, 72
Assassins 29
Ataide, E. de 76
Atlantic 11, 12
Aviz 12
Axim 12
Azevedo, C. de 9
Azores 11

Barboso, A. de 28
Barracks 23, 40, 42, 48
Bastions 21–23, 25, 28, 30–33, 40, 45, 52, 54, 74–77
Battlements 36, 45
Blockade 27, 54

Boarding 12
Boiler repairs 49
Bombardment 29
Bombay 14
Boxer, C. R. 9–11
Brazil 13, 14
Breastwork 75–77
Bridge 15
Bridges, R. 10
Britain 14, 29, 40, 41, 42, 53
Burial ground 76
Bwana, O. 10

Cabeceira 73
Cairato, João 19, 20, 21, 22, 23
Canaries 11
Cannibal 19, 55
Cannon 12–16, 24, 25, 32, 35, 40, 42, 64–66, 77
Cannonballs 42, 66
Cape 14, 73
Cape Verde Islands 11
Captains' house 23, 40, 43, 47
Captains of Mombasa 22, 23, 24, 25, 28
Captain of the Coast 24
Carronade 64, 65
Car parking 40
Castles 15
Catholic 11, 13, 14
Causeway 30, 38
Cavaliers 23, 25, 27, 28, 32, 35, 66
Caves 33
Ceuta 11
Ceylon 13
Chapel 76, 77
China 13
China Sea 13
Chingulia, Dom J. 24
Christian 11, 12, 18, 24, 25, 27, 58, 59
Church 23, 40

Cistern 23, 40, 77
Cochin 15
Coconut frond roof 43
Colonial powers 29, 56
Coral 19, 21, 24, 32, 33, 35, 36, 40, 44, 54, 58
Counterscarp 24, 33
Courtyard 19, 23, 29, 38, 40, 45, 77
Covered way 16, 52, 53
Cross-fire 54
Curator 9, 10
Curator's house 40, 66
Cutting 35

Daman 28
Daud, Prince 27
Defendable wall 36
Detached forts 54
Diamonds 13
Dias, Bartholeme 12
Disease 27, 28, 54
Ditch 15, 21, 23, 24, 28, 29, 30, 31, 32, 33, 34, 40, 52, 53, 54, 77
Diu 15, 28
Dominicans 14
Drawbridge 15, 38
Dutch 10, 13, 14, 15, 26, 64, 76

Earth-work 15, 16
East Africa 50, 58, 62
Education Officer 10
Egyptian 12
El-Kasr-el-Kebir 13
Elliptical extension 23, 25, 30, 31, 38, 47
Empire 11, 12, 13, 14, 18, 26, 73
English 18, 54, 64
Entry passage 19, 38
Esplanade 36
Ethiopia 62
Europe 11, 12, 51, 54, 56, 73
Execution 76

Faces 25, 31, 32, 33, 34, 36, 38, 47, 75
Faza 27
Ferry 58
Field of fire 19, 35
Fire-power 23, 25
Firestep 48, 76
First World War 49
Flag 38
Flanks 23, 24, 25, 31, 32, 33, 47, 74, 75

Fort George 53, 54
Fort S. Sebastian 73–77
Forts 14–16, 19
Foxhole, *see* Raposeira
France 64
Franciscans 14
French fleet 53
Frigate 28
Fruit market 56

Galleys 12
Gama, Vasco da 12, 56, 58, 59
Garrison 16, 21, 23, 28, 29, 52, 54
Gatehouse 25, 28, 40, 44, 47
Gates 15, 20, 23, 24, 25, 30, 31, 35, 38, 47, 48, 60, 73, 77
Gedi 56, 60–63
German 29, 49
Glacis 15, 52, 53
Goa 13, 15, 18, 22, 24, 25, 27, 28, 51, 73
Gold 12–14
'Great siege' 27, 28
Guard room 40
Guinea 12
Gulbenkian Foundation 25, 38
Gun carriage 52, 77
Gun-embrasures 24, 25, 31, 32, 33, 34, 35, 47, 49, 67–68, 76, 77
Gun Platform 19, 22, 23, 25, 49, 52
Gunpowder 12, 15, 28

Half-bastions 19, 21, 22, 23, 25, 28, 30, 33, 34, 35, 37, 38, 40, 45, 47, 49
Harlech Castle 54
Henry, Prince 12
Hindu 15, 58
Horse trade 13
Hughes, Quentin 10

Iberian Peninsula 11
India 12–15, 18, 28, 54, 59
Indian Ocean 12, 13, 14, 15, 17, 18, 24, 28, 29, 51, 73
Indonesia 13
Inscription 20, 38
Inverness 53
Iron grille 38, 62
Islam 44, 58

Japan 13
Jiddah 25

Jesuits 14, 76
Jungle 60

Kassim 60
Kenya 9, 10, 14, 29, 38, 41, 55
Kerimba 73
Kilifi 58
Kilindini harbour 19, 23, 27
Kilwa 14
King (Portuguese) 13, 24, 59
Kirkman J.S. 9, 10, 60, 73, 77
Kitchen 47
Koenigsberg 49, 50
Koran 44

Latrine tower 33
Lavatory 47
Light cruiser 49
Lingua franca 14
Lisbon 12, 13, 24, 40, 73
Litter 56, 58
Local levies 26
Loopholes 32, 34, 46, 49, 67–68
Lourenço Marques 14, 73

Macao 13
Madeira 11
Makupa ford 19
Malabar Coast 12, 13
Malacca 13
Malaria 77
Malindi 24, 55, 56–60
Man-power 21
Marathas 15, 54
Master of Works 20
Mazrui 29, 43
Mazrui house 40, 42, 43, 47
Mediterranean 12
Merlons 46
Military assessments 51, 54
Military systems 25
Mining 21
Mir Ali Bey 18
Missionaries 14
Mombasa 9, 14, 18, 19, 22, 23, 24, 25, 27, 28, 29, 42, 43, 49, 55, 56–58, 60, 73
Money 13, 52, 54
Monitors 50
Monsoon 51
Moors 11

Moray Firth 53
Morocco 11, 13
Moslem 11–14, 18, 24, 25, 27, 58, 59
Mosque 57, 58
Mossural 73
Mozambique 13, 14, 18, 28, 73, 76
Muscat 15
Musengulos 24
Museum 9, 10, 28, 40, 42, 49
Musketeers 15
Musketry 25, 32, 34, 46, 49, 52
Mwinzagu, A. 10
Mysticism 11

Naval guns 49
North Wales 54

Offices 40
Oman 15, 17, 18, 27, 29, 54, 55
Ormuz 13
Outer tunnel 38
Outwork 21, 25, 35, 36, 40, 43
Outworks 29, 52, 53, 54

Palace 48, 60
Parapets 15, 19, 21, 23, 38, 40, 45, 48, 49
Parker, G. 10
Passage of Arches 40, 43
Passage to postern 40
Passage of Steps 40, 43
Pate 27
Pegasus 49, 50
Peninsular War 11
Pepper trade 15
Persian Gulf 13, 17
Philip I (of Portugal) 19, 22
Philip II 13, 18, 22
Pillar 59, 60, 62
Pirate 24, 25
Plague 27, 54
Plant, J. 10
Plaster 9, 21, 31, 34, 35, 40, 43
Poona 15
Portuguese 9, 10, 11, 12, 13, 14, 15, 17, 18, 19, 22, 23, 24, 25, 26, 27, 28, 29, 34, 40, 41, 48, 51, 53, 54, 55, 56, 58, 59, 60, 64, 65, 69, 70, 73
Portuguese-patois 14
Portuguese town 23, 48, 56
Powder-magazine 28

Prester John 12
Priest's house 23, 40
Priest, visiting 23
Prison 40, 42
Protectorate of East Africa 29, 42
Protestant 13

Ramming 12
Ramp 77
Rampart 21, 23, 31, 32, 33, 40, 42, 45–47, 48, 73, 74, 75
Raposeira 23
Ravelin 52, 53
Rectangular projection 19, 21, 23, 25, 35, 36, 40, 45
Red Fort 14, 73
Red Sea 13, 18, 24, 25, 29
Refreshment room 40
Relief fleets 27, 28
Religion 11, 12, 18, 27, 58
Rifled guns 54
Rifuji River 50
Rio de Janeiro 13
Rockets 52, 54
Rodriques, G. 20

Sailing ships 12, 13, 19, 24, 35
S Alberto 23, 31, 32, 33, 74
S Filipe 22, 23, 24, 25, 28, 30, 31, 74
S Lourenço 14
S Mateus 22, 24, 25, 28, 30, 33, 34, 35, 47, 49
S Matias 22, 23, 30, 36, 47
S Sebastian 10, 14, 73–77
Salients 23, 24, 28, 32, 34, 35, 38, 76
Sandy cove 21, 35
Senegal 12
Sentry-box 32, 33, 34, 36, 48, 69–70
Shakespeare 24
Shingle 53
Shop 40
Side exit 35
Sikhs 58
Slaves 12
Smoke-escape hole 49
Sofala 14, 73
Soutomaior, L. 28

Spain 13, 18, 23, 53
Spaniards 11, 12
Spice 13
Starvation 21, 27, 54
Steps 77
Straits of Gibraltar 11, 13
Sultans 24, 25, 29, 34, 38, 42, 48, 59, 60
Sunk wall 15
Surrender 27, 29, 54
Swahili 14, 27, 28
Swahili Coast 14, 18, 23, 24, 25, 28, 29, 55, 60
Sweden 64
Swivel gun 24

Tanganika 29
Tangier 14
Tanzania 14
Thirst 54
Ticket office 40, 48
Timber 13, 28
Toilets 40, 47
Tombs 62
Trade 11, 12, 13
Treasure 28
Turks 13, 18, 24, 29, 51

Vasconcelos, M. M. de 20, 22, 34
Venice 64
Vertical walling 21, 24, 31, 37
Viceroy (at Goa) 22, 24, 51
Viceroy (of Portugal) 23
Village 60

Walkway 48
War junks 13
Water 23, 40, 77
Well 23, 40, 62
Wellington 11
Winter cold 54
Women 13

Yacht club 58
Yusif 24, 25

Zambesi 13, 14, 76
Zanzibar 27, 29, 49, 50